2012
PRESS 53
OPEN AWARDS ANTHOLOGY

2012
PRESS 53
OPEN AWARDS ANTHOLOGY

EDITED BY KEVIN MORGAN WATSON

Press 53
Winston-Salem

Press 53, LLC
PO Box 30314
Winston-Salem, NC 27130

First Edition

Copyright © 2012 Press 53

All Rights Reserved. Copyright for individual poems and stories are
owned by the respective authors. Permission for reprint, in whole or in
part, of individual works must be obtained from the author by contacting
author directly. Permissions may also be requested through Press 53 at
editor@press53.com or at the above address.

ISBN: 978-1-935708-72-8

Printed on acid-free paper

CONTENTS

Short Story

Creative Nonfiction

Novella

A Note from the Editor

This anthology of poetry and stories contains the winning entries from the 2012 Press 53 Open Awards, our fifth annual writing competition. We received entries from 37 states and five foreign countries. The Press 53 Open Awards, as the name implies, is open to writers at all stages of their careers. Since we believe that poems and stories should have many lives, the contest is open to previously published works, so long as the author has the right to grant us permission to publish his or her entry should it win.

This year we offered prizes in five categories—Poetry (three poems judged as a group), Flash Fiction (up to 1500 words), Short Story (1501 to 5000 words), Creative Nonfiction (up to 5000 words), and Novella (12,000 to 25,000 words)—with publication in this anthology of our First Prize, Second Prize, and Honorable Mention winners in four categories, and First Prize in Novella.

We've also listed the finalists in each category, including a Special Mentions page for participants who had two or more entries that were finalists in one of more categories.

All judging in the Press 53 Open Awards is done blind. Participants are asked to submit their entry along with a cover sheet. The participant's name can only appear on the cover sheet, not the manuscript. As the entries are received, we assign a number to the cover sheet and the manuscript. We then log the information and file the cover sheet. Our judges see only a number on the manuscript and are asked to immediately disqualify any entry they recognize as written by a friend or colleague. When the judges submit their final choices, we get a list of numbers, which we then match up with the cover sheets.

Protecting the integrity of this competition is vital, since it is our goal for the Press 53 Open Awards to become recognized as a high literary honor.

Since this was our fifth year, we decided to celebrate by inviting Press 53 and *Prime Number Magazine* authors and editors serve as final judges. I want to thank Tom Lombardo, editor of Tom Lombardo Poetry Selections, for juding Poetry; Meg Pokrass, author of *Damn Sure Right* and host of our weekly and free 53-Word Story Contest with Meg Pokrass for judging Flash Fiction; Clifford Garstang, author of the award-winning *In an Uncharted Country* and *What the Zhang Boys Know*, and editor of our award-winning online journal *Prime Number Magazine*, for judging Short Story; Tracy Crow, author of *Eyes Right: Confessions from a Woman Marine* (Univ of Nebraska Press) and nonfiction editor for *Prime Number Magazine* for judging Creative Nonfiction; and Robin Miura, former novel and memoir editor for Press 53 for judging Novella.

All of our First Prize winners receive a $250 cash prize, and a personalized etched-glass award that displays the category, the judge's name, and the participant's name along with the title of the winning poems or story. Second Prize and Honorable Mention winners will receive a personalized certificate. It is our hope that these awards will be proudly displayed and will serve as a source of continued inspiration.

We want the *Press 53 Open Awards Anthology* to be a publication in which readers, writers, and other publishers discover new voices. We will certainly end up publishing books by some of the writers you find in this volume, and it is our hope that an appearance in this anthology will open doors for all of these fine writers.

We look forward to the 2013 Press 53 Open Awards, which will bring a few changes. Next year we will have five categories, with a $250 cash prize plus the etched-glass award for First Prize. Flash Fiction will be limited to 750 words, and we will re-introduce the Short-Short Story category, for stories of 751-2000 words. Since Press 53's focus is now on publishing quality poetry and short stories, we have decided to drop the Creative Nonfiction category. So next year's categories will be Poetry, Flash Fiction, Short-Short Story, Short Story, and Novella.

Finding and recognizing new voices is what the Press 53 Open Awards is all about. We hope to read your words this coming year.

Kevin Morgan Watson
Press 53

SPECIAL MENTIONS

Press 53 salutes the following writers who received recognition for two or more works in one or more categories.

Dominique Traverse Locke of Lebanon, VA
Poetry: First Prize and Finalist

Arthur Powers of Raleigh, NC
Flash Fiction: Finalist
Short Story: Finalist

POETRY

Judged by Tom Lombardo

First Prize: Dominique Traverse Locke of Lebanon, VA for "Quiet"; "Bedtime Story"; "The Goodbye Child"

Second Prize: Peg Bresnahan of Cedar Mountain, NC for "A Khmer's Scarf of One Thousand Functions"; "At the Cemetery in Green Bay"; "At the Sunny Ridge Retirement Center"

Honorable Mention: David Cazden of Lexington, KY for "Portrait of Time as an Old Woman"; "Storm"; "In the Shadow of Flight 5191"

2012
PRESS 53
OPEN AWARDS

Finalists:

Ronald Dzerigian of Los Angeles, CA for "They are Carrying Me into Earth"; "Church"; "Morning"

Kathleen Giugliano of Westwood, MS for "On Running into an Ex-Lover"; "Cubism"; "Closure"

Dominique Traverse Locke of Lebanon, VA for "The Second Afternoon of Your Visit"; "Stories I Tell"; "Night Poem"

Ellaraine Lockie of Sunnyvale, CA for "Waiting for Midnight"; "American Haibun"; "Ashes"

Gerardo Mena of Columbia, MO for "So I Was a Coffin"; "Painting the War Blue"; "The Spent"

Michael Rattee of Tucson, AZ for "Circus Furniture"; "Dry Spell"; "Driving to Work"

Quiet

Dominique Traverse Locke

First Prize
Poetry

The lost ones are like that,
so careful not to bother the living.

Can something be made from this pain?
I have stitched together a blanket from its pieces.

I would have wrapped you in this blanket,
closed your tiny eyes with kisses, and each night,

scraped the dark from my face to watch you sleep.
I would have given up dreaming to keep watching.

Now, the days pass by. Good days, but many of them
I miss us being one body, mothering blood and bone.

Bedtime Story

Dominique Traverse Locke

I pat my lap and the moon sits down.
It is difficult to describe, I say to the moon.
There is a moment of strange calm
when you realize you are no longer a mother.
Not that the moon understands, ever faithful
in her roundness, unlike my stomach, flat
as the line of the little once upon a time heartbeat.

The Goodbye Child

Dominique Traverse Locke

My love, my tenant, you hardly existed.
But I thought I saw you. It was night, and you were there
in the doorway – a little girl, dark hair pulled back
with a ribbon like a puritan, a yellow square shining
behind you. But the change came all at once. Red,
and you were gone. I grieved for you then,
as I had never done before.

A Khmer's Scarf of One Thousand Functions

Peg Bresnahan

Second Prize
Poetry

Woven with essence of heat,
rain, fumes of red dust, trace
of jasmine, it rests on your shoulders
like the arm of a friend.

Shade from the sun, sling for the baby,
sash, towel, swatter of bugs, buffer
on your head for heavy loads,
ballooning as you turn your back.

Four corners tied, it carries taro,
rice and dragonfruit. If the wind slips
between, loose around your head,
it flares and sways like a cobra.

Bury your lips, your nose in its folds.
Silk threads cover countless questions
about the corruption you see, filter
the words a spy must not hear.

At the Cemetery in Green Bay

Peg Bresnahan

I never knew where my son went
when he was supposed to be at North High.
Now he's dead
and I still can't find him.

I was just here a week ago
but I can't remember which tree,
trash can or water spigot he's near.

I've driven past lambs, angels, obelisks
and acres of graves—granite
two feet by three—just like his.

This place changes constantly.
Every time someone dies
it seems they add a gravel road.

I let Lou out of the car.
Dogs sense things.
After all she's a hound
and he had her five years.

We're the only ones alive
this morning. Lou with her nose
to the ground, tail wagging.
Me carrying a pail of pansies, sweet
alyssum and a trowel.

At the Sunny Ridge Retirement Center

Peg Bresnahan

During Harriet's memorial service,
Frances leaned, put her head
on my shoulder and died—quietly

as if she didn't want to interrupt
Harriet's program.
The minister didn't see us,

no one knew except me. At the piano,
Mary played the introduction
to *Going Home*. Everyone thumbed

their hymnals for page two hundred forty-three.
I didn't know what to do, since Frances
still looked like Frances, only not quite

and she was ninety-five. I put my arm
around her so she wouldn't fall
and waited for someone to notice.

Through the French doors
finches squabbled at the bird feeder.
The squirrel we call Rocky

contemplated his next move.
A laundry truck rolled by.
I looked down at Frances' navy blue crocs,

the ones she claimed felt so much
like bedroom slippers
she could wear them anywhere.

Portrait of Time as an Old Woman

David Cazden

Cradling a decanter
—cut sapphire crystal—

my grandmother would pour sherry,
rosining my vocal cords.

She'd paint calamine
like milk across red welts

of poison sumac on my arms.
I was twelve and out of school

when jazz dropped
on the console stereo

and the needle fell into the groove
July nights.

Music lifted through the hall
as I lay in bed

and her hands slid down my neck
like fingers on the banisters.

Now when I walk
on floral carpets,

past fleur-de-lis covered walls,
I find that hugging her

is like grasping a vase of lilacs,
stems thin and brittle,

that she's fragile as the rim
of an old LP. And all I hear

is the warning groove
at record's end,

ticking off and on
like steady breathing,

as if she's asking to be turned
to the other side.

Storm

David Cazden

I find a drowned bird
beneath a sewer grate:

neck pinched in, wings bent
against the flow.

So I pry the screen away,
lift him up, walk to my backyard,

crease the earth, and bury him.
Then I say a prayer

for things that fall to us,
back to the dirt and fast water.

I scan scattered leaves, newspapers
blown from porches, but see nothing more

among the branches
and roots exposed by flood.

So I go inside and call
to tell you what I found.

How the bird appeared, for a moment,
as if it could have been our own

unborn—returned
in a gale, swaddled by rain.

Yet your voice reminds me:
once we waited

in a fluorescent clinic,
then when everything was done,

how it felt,
as if all clouds had parted

as we walked into the streets
and through the clear, sharp air

which always remains
whenever the soil drowns

and streams overflow their banks,
their courses changed—by a storm.

In the Shadow of Flight 5191

David Cazden

7 am, on the runway at Blue Grass Field

Clutching my in-flight magazine,
I can see my own home
near Parker's Mill Road.

Even the curve of its driveway
where I'd usually walk,
stooping for the morning news.

But today, a hum of engines begins
behind me; sheets of air
lift over the wings.

In this same moment of take-off,
Flight 5191's hull
hurtled into the trees.

But I watch the ground fade, wondering
if Flight 5191 would've followed
these hills and fences,

this cross-hatch of farms and orchards,
if the crash hadn't happened,
if forty-nine passengers hadn't inhaled

sudden fumes, as jet fuel
rolled in a wave
over the grass, melting

seat cushions and stones,
bending layers of ash
from in-flight magazines

scattering a pumice of flesh.
So I sit back, attempt to relax
in the window seat, and watch

a journey through cloud,
listening to the turbines' tune
as the plane simply rises away.

FLASH FICTION

Judged by Meg Pokrass

First Prize: Art Taylor of Burke, VA
for "Mastering the Art of French Cooking"

Second Prize: Nahal S. Jamir of Tallahassee, FL
for "Foundling"

Honorable Mention: Amanda Pauley of Elliston, VA
for "Snapshot"

2012
PRESS 53
OPEN AWARDS

Finalists:

Katie Cortese of Tallahassee, FL for "History, Revised"

Gianna Jacobson of St. Louis, MO for "Compound Fracture"

Alexander Lumans of Boulder, CO for "The Dictionary of Your Fears"

Arthur Powers of Raleigh, NC for "Famine"

Jane Shlensky of Bahama, NC for "Dogs, Work"

Linda Wastila of Baltimore, MD for "The Abridged Biography of an American Sniper"

Mastering the Art of French Cooking

Art Taylor

First Prize
Flash Fiction

Coq au Vin

1 onion
2 carrots
2 stalks celery
6 whole peppercorns
2 cloves garlic, pureed
1 sprig parsley
1 bay leaf
¼ tsp thyme
3 bottles Burgundy (two inexpensive, one not)
2 Tbsp white arsenic (from the hardware store)
2 Tbsp sugar
1 whole chicken
Salt and pepper
2 Tbsp olive oil
4 Tbsp butter, divided
1 Tbsp flour
1 ripe red tomato
¼ lb lardons (or thick bacon, cut into small strips)
½ pound mushrooms

With a sharp knife, dice onions and slice carrot and celery into small discs. Avoid cutting yourself. Combine onions, carrots, celery, peppercorns and garlic into a large bowl. Tie parsley, bay leaf and thyme into a small cheesecloth to make a *bouquet garni*; add to mixture. Douse with one bottle of wine, reserving approximately one swallow. Stir gently.

Look at the mixture. Slug the rest of the wine from the bottle.

Add the next ingredient.

Then add the next, to ease the bitterness.

Reflect on that word *bitterness*.

With a sharp knife, gut the chicken, trim away the neckbone and wing tips, and carve it into manageable pieces: breasts, legs, thighs, etc. Admire the sharpness of the knife, how easily it slides through the meat. See how it gleams. Feel your grip tighten. Listen to the sound of the television in the next room. Consider for a moment the alternatives. You've considered them before.

Submerge the chicken in the bowl of vegetables and seasonings. Hold it down tight.

The preceding stage of the recipe may be completed a day in advance. In fact, such a delay is preferred for superior taste and enriched texture. Cover the bowl tightly with plastic wrap and refrigerate.

Overnight and throughout the next day, reflect on the art of French cooking, a mix of sophistication and heartiness, style and romance. Consider how Julia Child brought these qualities into the early '60s suburban home — a sense of wonder at the wider world, a hint of possibility, as if anybody could do it.

Question why *French Women Don't Get Fat*.

Browse the internet for photos of Emmanuelle Béart, Isabelle Adjani, Marion Cotillard, Sophie Marceau, Audrey Tautou. While on the computer, scan your husband's email once or twice more, searching for the name Monique. Look at the picture she sent him, the high cheekbones, the creamy complexion, the glimpses of skin.

Reflect once more on that word *bitterness*.

Browse through several of the other words in this recipe: *ripe,*
bouquet, leg, thigh, breast, stalk. Know that *coq* simply means *chicken,*
but laugh inwardly at what it sounds like. Think about it: *coq* in
wine. Understand where drunkenness can lead.

Open the second bottle of wine and have a couple of glasses,
since you'll only use a cup of it later.

Ponder the word *lardons.* Regret your love of bacon. Glance
down at your own thighs.

Two hours in advance of dinner, remove the chicken from the
vegetable marinade and put aside. Strain the marinade, separating
liquids and solids, and reserve each. Set aside the *bouquet garni.*

Heat oil and half the butter in a large Dutch oven over medium-
high heat. Salt and pepper the chicken. Sear quickly and evenly
until brown. Look at how the skin sizzles. Consider for a moment
the alternatives. Remove from heat and set aside.

Add the reserved vegetables to the pot and cook, stirring
occasionally, until browned. Sprinkle with flour, mix gently, then
add reserved marinade. Return chicken to the pot. Dice and add
the tomatoes. Toss in the *bouquet garni.* Remember tossing the
bouquet at your own wedding. Remember an earlier wedding
when you caught it yourself and gave a sly glance at the man
you'd ultimately marry. Recall how happy you were. Resist
sampling this mixture, no matter how appetizing it seems.

Cook over low heat for an hour and a half. Have more of that
second bottle of wine, careful to reserve at least a cup for later.
Watch the clock.

Lardons! You almost forgot! Conveniently, yes? As if. (Look at
your thighs again.)

Cook the lardons in a small skillet over medium heat until crisp.

Remove them to a plate lined with paper towels, reserving bacon fat. Add mushrooms and cook until browned. Gauge the weight of the skillet. Gauge the heat of the grease. Consider for a moment more alternatives. Add the reserved cup of wine to the bacon fat and deglaze the pan. Set the skillet aside.

When the chicken is tender and cooked through, add the bacon, mushrooms, and red wine glaze to the Dutch oven. Swirl in the remaining butter. Season with more salt and pepper — but *not* to taste, no matter how tempting a taste might be and for so many reasons. Resist dramatic exits, overt melodrama, sentimentalizing. A single tear? Well, if you insist. There's loss here, after all, for everyone. Just stir it in quickly, so no one sees.

Hear your husband say, "Something smells good" as he comes through the door. Watch him smile guilelessly. Ask how his day was. Don't believe anything he tells you.

Serve *coq au vin* warm over noodles or rice along with crusty French bread and the third bottle of Burgundy, the one your husband picked up for "some special occasion." When he sees it and asks if this is indeed a special occasion, try to muster something witty, such as, "Isn't every day a special occasion with me?" or "If one's going to enjoy a French meal, one simply *must* go all the way," or perhaps even a jaunty "Vive la France!" Try not to lace your words with sarcasm.

Consider that word *lace*. Picture the frilly underthings you assembled as a surprise for your honeymoon. Hear your mother calling it a *trousseau* and remember savoring the word. Imagine Monique in a push-up bra and a g-string. Consider the purpose of a *corset*. Consider the phrase *merry widow*.

At the last moment, beg off eating yourself. He knows how you've been lately about saturated fats. Or maybe a sudden headache and you've lost your appetite. It's more important that he enjoy it. Really any excuse will do. But yes, you'll sit with him and have some wine.

Then discover why you went to all this trouble. Hear him tell you how delicious it is. Hear him say, "What a long way from chicken and dumplings, isn't it, hon?" Hide your surprise that he remembers the first meal you made for him. Hide your surprise when he shakes his head and laughs and admits, "Good as this is, it just can't compete with those dumplings." See him recognize what he's saying.

Remember how he carried you across the threshold. Picture dancing in the living room, just the two of you, alone on a Saturday night, head on shoulder, hand on hip. Examine the crow's feet at the corners of his eyes.

In the middle of all that, change your mind. Serve yourself a plate too.

Because marriage is about being in it together, isn't it? For better or worse?

And perhaps this isn't a melodramatic exit, but a stylish one — sophisticated even, romantic in its own way.

Toast him graciously.

Smile warmly, sincerely.

Pick up your fork and knife.

Take that first bite.

Foundling

Nahal S. Jamir

Second Prize
Flash Fiction

She is born in curtains, curtains with a pattern of flowers and curtains that feel like flowers but smell clean, like midnight from her second-story bedroom window. These curtains, they aren't thin like paper. That's what a smarter girl would say. These curtains, they are thin like flower petals. Try looking through a flower petal. And this is how she first sees her mother, on a leather recliner that creaks and moans. This is her mother, silent.

Her mother is gone now, left them for some other city far away. Noise fills the house because of her father, a tall man with hair that crackles when he runs his hands through it. He cries and yells at the ceiling. He throws food into the sink and then lets the garbage disposal run too long. Empty metal clanging.

Finally, one day, he stops the noise and brings the young girl out from the curtains. "What are you doing there?" he asks. And when she doesn't answer: "Well, I've got you now. We're going to be okay." A smarter girl would not have believed him.

The envelope says *overdue*, like library books. She got her own library card a month ago. She reads stories about old things, like swords and magic and large trees. These make her feel safe. She reads and the house is quiet but the words loud in her head where the dragon and dragon-rider bond and kill danger. Where the magician saves the princess. Where a stone is not a stone, a flower not a flower.

The envelope is new, thin like paper. The girl opens it because she knows how to take care of overdue library books. Inside, a large bill for what are called *utilities*. Water, gas, electricity. Just add wind, she thought, and you'd have all of the elementals. She's read about elementals. Without wind, or any one, the elementals wobble out of balance.

For a while, her mother's things disappeared. They return now as the girl turns thirteen. An eight-by-ten picture of her mother sits on the scratched dining room table, next to a vase of tall flowers. A feminine jacket, practical but almost as soft as velvet, hangs on a brass hook next to the front door. If the light shines through the side window just right, the girl can see the holes her mother darned. Don't let anything in, her mother used to say in the winter months. Her mother's voice on the answering machine, asking you to call back. Come back. Backwards motion picks up speed. Her thirteenth birthday races toward her from long-ago, and she braces herself with all she can find.

Something has changed. Her father spends hours in the bathroom. Most nights, when she asks, he says he is praying.

Tonight, she knocks and he doesn't answer, so she picks the lock with a paperclip, and there he is, silent. He clings to himself and sighs in response to her questions. The pungency of rubbing alcohol. He has written "see her die again" in permanent marker and then tried to scrub it out. She can't leave. A piece of her father's crackly hair has fallen onto the counter. The girl places it on her thumb, blows and makes a wish. A smarter girl would have cried.

She's on her first date wearing a thin dress. Here is a boy with light hair and full-round eyes. He asks serious questions. They both stare at their plates as she tells him about her mother leaving. The whole time, the boy holds her hand and puts light pressure on the veins, one at a time. Does this make her blood stop? He doesn't ask questions about her father, and she decides she will fall in love with this boy. A smarter girl would have.

On the way to the car, he picks her a pink azalea. She can feel his hand through her dress. And she wonders if this is how it begins. If this is how you forget to protect yourself from sadness, how you forget to leave your child with a kind shepherd. But then, the boy kisses her, and she is back in that garden of clean flowers, watching.

Snapshot

Amanda Pauley

Honorable
Mention
Flash Fiction

A shot fired and the half-open front window glass shattered as the bullet came through the far end of my room and went on through the wall. There it hit the top of a framed painting of a nude woman reclining in the grass at the bank of a creek next to a covered bridge while a man on a horse watched her from the other side with an angry expression. Frame and all dropped straight to the floor on its edge and then went face down.

A friend of mine had made the painting for me. She gave it to me to thank me for letting her borrow my car. After she returned the car it had a strange smell for over a week. I kept my mouth shut because I liked the gift so much, maybe even a little more than I liked her. I knew what that smell was, just like I knew the shot that had just been fired through the upstairs of the house which I rented from my father who lived downstairs, was not for me, but for him, not for killing anyone, just for scaring.

Although the noise itself startled me, I was not surprised at a bullet flying through the air after thirty-five years of surprises, so I finished the last bite of my soy taco, set the dish in the sink, and went to the window to look at the man standing in my yard with a rifle. His green baseball hat sat up on top of his head and gave him a stupid look. There was not much danger in being at the window now because he was watching my father's small cow herd. The shot had sent the herd on a miniature stampede.

The cows ran a circle around the field twice while I and the stupid man in the yard watched. When they slowed closer to the house you could see the creatures breathing deeply. Some had a froth of spit around the mouth and most still seemed uneasy. One female mounted another and I thought how strange it was that after thirty-five years my father still had not realized that I was gay. Telling him was beside the point because he did not *believe* in gay.

"He's not home!" I yelled toward the man with the green hat. He looked like the kind of man a woman's voice could scare off. "Now get off the property before I call the police!" I waived a cell phone around for show and then watched as he turned around and walked down the driveway. The cows were calming down and some started to chew their cud again.

I picked up the painting. It would need to be reframed, but the painting was still intact. The woman's eyes were calm and seemed to be watching something outside of the painting's view. I liked the scene because it was lovely, if a little dark. Not a rare or precious moment, but a moment worth capturing.

SHORT STORY

Judged by Clifford Garstang

First Prize: Kathryn Etters Lovatt of Camden, SC
for "How to Euthanize a Fish"

Second Prize: Alison Morse of Minneapolis, MN
for "The Truth About 'The Lead Plates at the Romm Press':
A Lecture by Abraham Sutzkever"

Honorable Mention: Gary Powell of Cornelius, NC for
"Super Nova"

Finalists:

Susannah Cecil of Clemmons, NC for "Their Crazy"

Gregg Cusick of Durham, NC for "Ghosts of Doubt"

Tom Mock of Moncure, NC for "Moon Song"

Arthur Powers of Raleigh, NC for "The Bridge"

Russell Reece of Bethel, DE for "The the Marshfield Dam"

Michael Twist of Boring, OR for "Out on a Limb"

Marion de Booy Wentzien of Saratoga, CA for "The Art of
Disappearing""""

How to Euthanize a Fish

Kathryn Etters Lovatt

First Prize
Short Story

Three, maybe four nights a week, I still head out to Wong's.

When the weather's right and it's not too late, I kick my pumps into the closet and tie on my walkers. The fat girl inside me favors the unbroken sidewalk along the thoroughfare, but I like the back way. There's laurel there, a sweep of evergreens. Rhododendrons grow right into the mouth of the pedestrian tunnel. Sometimes an old man sits inside, his back to the concrete, legs hugged close. He greets everybody as they come along.

"Have a blessed day," he calls to passers-by or "peace be with you." No matter what he says, most of us keep moving.

But one evening, back when the year felt relatively new instead of nearly half over, he uncrossed his long legs and shoved them directly in my path. I had to stop or stumble. Draped for winter, he looked like an ancient shag oak, and he smelled not exactly dirty, but like dirt itself.

"I'm nobody," he said and stuck out a gray felt hat. Inside was an orange, two waters and a postcard of DC in bloom. "Who are you?"

I fumbled through my purse and came up with a box of raisins that rattled like pinto beans. I added them to his collection anyway.

"T'is brillig." He pulled up his knees and cleared the way. "Beware the jabberwock."

That was before I knew about jabberwocks or their burblings or even about fish, but his outburst sent me high-tailing through what remained of the tunnel. When I came out into the yellow vapors of strip mall parking, I kept up my pace. One more turn at the corner and the bright red glow of Wong's sign came into view. Even with the interruption, I'd made door-to-door in seventeen minutes flat. I can't get in my car and drive into downtown Reston any faster.

However I get to Wong's, I walk in and find a place around the massive Lazy Susan. A wide conveyor belt carries along a stream of small dishes, but not only sushi. Ellis and the other chefs, who work in full view, labor to keep a surprise or two on the loop. Pad Thai might show up, Singapore noodles, curry or pho and once, a rendang so spicy hot, they gave it away.

Everyone at the counter falls into the same rhythm, taking one item at a time and stacking empties like nesting blocks in the spaces between tea cups and dipping bowls. A raised hand gets the attention of Ernesto, who constantly roams the exterior of the bar. With a nod of his head or a snap of his fingers, he sends a runner to count color-coded plates, present bills and hand over a fortune cookie. Twice, my cookie had no message in it at all.

Sometimes, if the place is too crazy for Ellis to come over to say hello, Ernesto might bring me take-away. I wave thanks to Ellis and give up my spot. Restaurants like Wong's want customers in and out, and they want a lot of them. No time to check messages. No space for a laptop. You get about the same amount of wiggle room as flying coach. As a result, elbow-to-elbow dining has hatched a set of manners, the golden one being *keep to yourself.* So if a week or two roll by before you realize you're regularly handing low-sodium soy sauce or the wasabi pot to the exact same person, that's not a mark of indifference, it's a sign of respect.

That night, the same night I got blocked in the tunnel, I did notice the man to my left. He started with seaweed salad and moved to unagi. He took a dish of miso prawns, a bundle of asparagus, melon. After that, I began to see how he nearly always found a place on one side of me or the other. Ernesto noticed, too, and brought the check himself before the stranger ever waved his hand.

My neighbor wore no wedding band. As a consequence, a tube of cherry lip gloss found its way into my pocket. I had my hair cut and styled and scattered with golden highlights. I bought black suede gloves, citrine earrings, a red cashmere scarf the saleswoman promised would last forever. Should others claim the seats beside me, I felt the disappointment, and if my companion never came at all, I succumbed to the sweet goo of mochi cakes. The first week of March, when he was a no-show five times in a row, my weight went up one pound, two ounces. I gave myself a good talking to: who was this man anyway, and what was he to me that I should be eating my way off Weight Watchers' maintenance and back into stretch jeans? But when I walked in on the sixth night, a rush of pleasure swelled over me. Even in low lighting, I recognized him from the back. His shoulders squared his jacket, as if the suit was custom-tailored, and his hair-dark and course, the exact opposite of mine-conformed and disobeyed in all the right places. I knew how he would smell too, like autumn leaves and wormwood. The minute I sat down, he spoke.

"I love the pickled ginger here." He balanced a slice, pure white instead of the common pink variety, between the points of his chopsticks.

"Me, too," I agreed before I gave myself a chance to think.

The very next night, I trudged through a cold mist in hopes of seeing him. The old man, his legs rolled out like logs, sat parked in the tunnel. I hadn't seen him since the raisins.

"Don't stand there in uffish thought," he said. "What'd you bring me?"

"Sugar free mints?" I held them up.

He shook his head. "Poison."

I rambled around in my purse. "Granola bar?"

"Not a good tooth in my head." He opened his mouth and showed me. "You have two dollars?"

I handed him four bills, folded over. He gave two back and motioned me on. "Snicker-snack!" he said. "And take the vorpal sword in hand."

"Vorpal, vorpal, vorpal." I committed the word to memory as I walked to Wong's

When I got there, I hesitated at the door and seriously thought about going over and edging in between two guys too big for their stools. But I didn't.

"Just so you know," he said once I settled. "I don't bite."

What I knew was that he looked even better full-on than out of the corner of my eye. I figured him to be two inches taller than me, five-feet-ten, late thirties I guessed, not even a decade between us, but, from the way things appeared, he'd taken that time to grow smooth and handsome and successful.

"I'm not trying to be rude," I apologized, "but you could be a serial killer."

"You're smart to be careful." He picked up my cup and motioned to Ernesto. Ernesto ignored him. "But now that we've spoken, I've been wondering, just how spicy is that spicy tuna?"

A question like that, I can tell you, requires an entire conversation.

"David," he said at the end of it. "David Perry."

"Mabry."

He licked his lips after he repeated my name, like he was trying to taste the sound he'd made. "I'll bet there's a story that goes along with that."

And before I finished my dragon roll, he'd gotten more of it than he bargained for.

I told him where I was from and where I lived and all about my MBA. He heard what my fancy degree earned me: good money, a cubicle in a maze of cubicles, promises a city makes. He even knew my pinkie ring had belonged to my great grandmother, a Mabry from the narrow stretch of land claimed by both Carolinas. I gave up everything save my social security number. Once I had talked beyond reason, I was set to listen.

"What about you?"

"I'm a government consultant." He folded his napkin.

"Ah," I said and shifted my attention to a pair of shrimp dumplings.

It didn't take much silence for him to bring out the broad smile, his teeth a shade shy of too-white. "All right," he said. "Tit for tat. What if I told you that I gathered information?"

When he shifted in his place, drawing closer, his knee brushed my knee. A current went through me.

"What kind of information?"

"Sensitive information. Need-to-know information."

"Are you saying you're some kind of spy?"

"I'm not saying that." He leaned toward me. "I'm saying I'm a consultant."

"Well, whatever you do, I expect you're good at it. The Westin comes at a price."

"And what makes you so sure I'm at The Westin?"

"Gold Rolex." The watch sat low on the hump of his wrist, face to the inside.

He ran his finger along the band. "Could be a fake."

"Then you'd be staying at Comfort Inn, and Wong's is a long way from there."

"Actually, I find one hotel room is pretty much like the next."

"One luxury hotel room maybe. So, where's home?"

"Boston, I guess." He shrugged with just the right dash of torment. "My offices are there, and I own a property."

Who says such a thing, that they own "a property"? But, at that point, I had already unplugged my shit detector. Sharing edamame with a secret agent who vanished to carry out clandestine missions: that was a page-turner. My own everyday story consisted largely of charts and numbers.

Through the rest of March, the two of us met weeknights at Wong's. We talked about DC traffic and violent crime, suburban blight and urban angst. In that entire time, the man in the tunnel had nothing to say to me. All he did was put a finger to his lips and go, "Shhh."

I told David about him, how he was a puzzle I never expected to solve. He ordered saki and poured a thimbleful for each of us. A pale sip cooled in my mouth and warmed up again when I swallowed.

"You can't help people who don't want help," said David.

"Who would those people be?"

"The ones who just want a hand-out."

"Or need a hand-out. That's what we call compassion, right?"

"Tomorrow night," he replied, "let's go out for a proper meal."

I hesitated.

"And why not?"

"Because it's cozy in here, and it's crazy out there."

"You like Italian?"

So our big date would be Osso Bucco for two at Rossi's, pretty heavy after so many dinners of mostly raw fish and rice. A split of wine helped break the meal down, and it loosened my tongue. I wasn't finished with my conversation from the night before.

"You know that man in the tunnel I told you about? I never pass him by that I don't leave some little offering, but he barely gives a nod in my direction."

"Maybe he's playing you. Have you considered that? He's found that ignoring you is the best way to get your attention."

"It's not only me who pays attention to him. He has what you might call a presence."

"Mabry, sweetheart, don't kid yourself. There's a hard luck prophet at every turn."

"I never said he was a prophet."

"Believe you me, it's a well-wrought scam. He's working up to something."

"I don't feel scammed." My voice stretched an octave. "I always feel glad to see him. Glad to be greeted or hear his riddles. And now that he's ignoring me, I feel let down. Or like I let him down."

David reached over and patted my hand. "You're such an innocent."

I longed suddenly for the familiar boundaries of Wong's, where David was in his space instead of moving into mine.

"You sound like my mother." I pulled my hand away. "She's always worrying about scoundrels and muggers and whether I've got my pepper spray in my pocket."

"I have absolutely no desire to mother you." The way he said it made me look away.

The table cleared, he paid cash, as usual, and came over to pull out my chair.

"Are you going to let me drive you home?" I had insisted we meet, cautious to the end. "I have a surprise," he said, steering me outside, across the street and into the parking garage. The box in the backseat of his glossy rental was tall enough for a plumed hat to fit inside. A safety belt held it in its place. David glided right past me when I opened the door to my condo. The night before, I'd stayed up cleaning, just in case. He eased the box onto my gleaming kitchen counter.

"Is it a cake?"

He patted the flat of his stomach. "I don't eat cake."

"Never?"

"Never."

That was another long, loud fingernail scratch across the chalkboard. You can bet on it: a man who does not eat cake will not want you to eat cake either.

But right then, he pulled me over to kiss the curve of my neck with such familiar intimacy, I was ready to renounce dessert forever. Plus, that box blunted my instincts almost as much as the wet heat of his lips. A bouquet of ribbons ran over the sides and gathered in a green and white spill. I parted them like seaweed, loosened the container's corners, and shook off the top.

Sheet upon sheet of pastel tissue concealed and cushioned what lay hidden inside. I dug down and lifted out a glass bowl long as my elbow to wrist. It was shaped, as far as I could tell, like a wide-mouth bass. Inside, I found a small net, food flakes; one pack of red hearts, another of clear marbles. At the bottom, in a Ziplock, quivering in the ladle of water he'd been dipped out with, was David, the fish. Although, technically, he was not yet David.

"He's a Siamese fighting fish. He'll charge his reflection in a mirror. And Bettas are freshwater tropicals, easy care. Fish food and clean water and you're good-to-go."

"For a travelling man, you sure know a lot about fish."

"Not much you need to know. That's the beauty of it."

When I brought the bag to eye level, my fish flared like a miniature peacock. He spread his fin into a dazzle of blue and red feathers. He didn't back off when I drew him closer.

"Well, hello," I said to him.

"His name is Khan."

Straight away, David shucked off his jacket and hung it on a chair. He rolled up the starched sleeves of his shirt as if he were a surgeon, but he wasn't fast enough. The block letters on his cuff were thick and black and easy to read. Not a 'D' or a 'P' in the bunch. I watched silently as he spread the glass in the bottom of the bowl. The pieces rearranged themselves under the force of the tap, tumbling in the wake, pinging like gravel on a windshield. He floated the bagged fish on top of the water in the bowl and thumped the plastic with a finger. Khan puffed up twice his normal size and flared his colors.

"We'll leave him there tonight. The water in the bag and the water in his bowl need to reach the same temperature. Otherwise, he might die of shock." He gave a double pump to the hand soap at the sink and worked the lather up his forearms. "In the morning," he said, never missing a beat, "we'll move him to his new home."

I took one of those balancing Yoga breaths: in through the nose, hold, woosh through a puckered mouth. "I have a rough day tomorrow," I said. "And it's Friday. You'll be going to Boston. Or wherever it is you're really from."

He finished drying his hands on my red checked towel before he turned to face me. He leaned his back against the lip of the sink.

"The monogram?"

I stood there, arms folded.

"It might not mean what you think."

I could have stopped traffic, the way my hand snapped up. "Don't." I didn't want more lies any more than I wanted the truth. I didn't want to hear about what he did, why he was here, who he was. If I had his name or any trace of a clue, I knew that, in a weak moment, I would get on the computer and dig.

He looked me over without a fragment of shame. "You knew. Admit it. You had to know. And you played along."

His accusation stung me. I was a fool or he was right, or, worse, both.

He took a step closer. "Does it honestly matter? I like you. You like me. Here we are."

"What do you want to do about your fish?"

"Come on, Mabry, be reasonable. We can work this out."

I shifted into full business-mode, straightening the set of my spine. I know how to conduct a meeting, and I know how to end one. "Don't forget your coat," I said, handing it to him. "And stay clear of Wong's."

David spun the jacket around his finger and flipped it over his right shoulder. "One thing you were right about," he said at the door. "I *could* have been a serial killer."

Lucky me.

Next morning, I called in sick.

Because I had not so much as a cake crumb in the pantry, I breakfasted on peanut butter and Coke before I stomped the pretty white box flat. Tissue, curling ribbons, cardboard, the balled up kitchen towel: everything went to the garbage bin. I tried not to fault Khan, still cramped in temporary quarters.

He flowed from bag to bowl without making a wave. Now, I would have to figure out how to care for him, and, frankly, I didn't want to spend a speck more energy on fictional men or real fish.

"Damn you, David," I said, and the fish darted around to me as if I'd dangled a worm. "David," I said again and, I swear, he bobbed. I drew a barstool to the kitchen counter and put my cheek down on the cool granite slab. The dimmest light travelled up and down David's scales, and he could glide or still himself with an iridescent swish. I pulled the bowl over and he fit himself to the glass like a hand against a mirror.

All morning, I stayed there. Didn't matter the blinds were shut, that no music played, that a cabinet door stood ajar. I stared at the fish and he stared back. His right eye seemed to bulge more than the left. The illusion of convex glass, I thought, and tapped in a few more fish flakes.

"It wasn't love," I said aloud. "Not yet." David circled beneath the morsels, rose and swallowed each one before he came back to me. The upturned slit of his mouth drew his nubby teeth into a benevolent smile.

In the back of my freezer, a frozen enchilada, bought the first week I'd moved here, sat in a snowy corner. I banged off seven months of accumulated ice and threw the package in the microwave. Over lunch, I pulled over the computer and ran a search on Bettas. David, I found, had already consumed many times over his recommended daily portion. And he ought to have a plant, both to hide behind and to hold his bubble nests of air. I flipped the screen and showed him a picture of another Betta Splendens. He rushed forward like a shark.

"No wonder you have no friends." I shut down the program and David, decompressed to standard size, swam a few wild circles before coming back to rest in front of me. "Better?" I asked, and we went from there.

For weeks, I mostly complained. I grumbled about the Yorkie next door, the smell of garlic oozing through my vents, how long it took to find your way into a new place. I talked about work, where snap- together pods linked everyone together and glass partitions kept everyone apart. My father was right, I had to admit, there was nothing on television. I bitched so much about this and that, David's colors began to fade.

A month in, he stopped showing off for his dinner. In the beginning, he went round and round while I ate grilled cheese, eggs on toast, cup noodles and read *Through the Looking Glass*. When I fed him his bits now, he showed no interest at all. The pellets sat on the top of the water, then fell heavily and slowly toward the bottom of the bowl. That old bulge, which seemed more sinister than before, began to worry me.

"Popeye probably," said the man at the pet store. "Common ailment with Bettas. Add this to the water."

I bought a treasure chest and mosquito larvae to see if anything would make him rally. He didn't seem to notice when I dropped them in, and I could tell from the way he stayed on the other side of the bowl, he wanted to be left alone.

I put a V-8 in one pocket and Cheese Doodles in the other. The woods were full of May.

"Where've you been?" demanded the old man in the tunnel.

"Where've you been?"

"Back in the stacks." He curled the stump of an index finger around the V-8's pop top and lifted. "Gyring and gimbling in the wabe."

"Jabberwocky." My mention of the poem interested him less than the snack bag. He tore open a corner of the package and dropped one bright orange curl in his mouth. "Lewis Carroll."

He tapped his head. "You put on your thinking cap," he said and went back to eating.

"You need anything?"

He shut his eyes and squinched as if he might have left a shopping list under his lids. "Can't say that I do." He handed me a Cheese Doodle.

"Thank you." I popped the piece in my mouth.

"Go," he said. "Plant your nine bean rows."

When I walked into the sushi bar, the staff greeted me with two claps. The three mostly Japanese chefs yelled, "Moshi-moshi" with genuine enthusiasm. Ernesto grabbed the pot of green tea.

"You okay?" The tea gurgled into my cup.

"Fine," I said, hoping to move past the fact that it had been more than a month since I'd shown my face.

"Wong's been worried sick over you."

"He has?" I looked to the middle. "Which one is he?"

"Ellis," said Ernesto, shaking his head in frustration.

"Ellis is Wong?"

"There is no real Wong, chiquita. There's only Ellis."

"God," I said. "Maybe nobody's who you think they are."

He grabbed a plate and put it in front of me. "Rice paper wrapped around tempura shrimp. We can't keep them on the line."

I could see why. Ellis had outdone himself. *Ellis: Funny*, I thought, throwing him a smile. Everyone was a mystery. And some were jabberwocks and bandersnatches, but most, I had to believe, were not. We lived in the world all alone, all together, trying to make sense of our lives.

"Where's your friend?" Ernesto asked when he came back around.

"At the moment, my best friend happens to be a fish."

"Yeah?" He reached in his pocket and brought out a Starlight mint. "You better eat this then, before you get home."

The candy didn't last the first block as I walked the longer, well-lit way back to my complex. When I went in and turned on the light, no flutter came from the direction of my counter. I went closer. David looked like a ship on its side. His bad eye had turned into a kernel of corn. Before I called the pet store, I knew he was a goner, but I had to try.

"Doesn't sound good," said the man on the phone when I told him the symptoms.

"But I thought they lived for years."

"How old was he when you bought him, do you know that? And where did he come from? Not every shop cares for their stock."

I felt sick at heart. And responsible. Had I changed his water enough or changed it too much? Maybe those blood worms had stuck in his craw.

"Is there nothing I can do?"

"Not let him suffer. A lot of people put them down the toilet."

But one website, which provided a vivid description of a flushed fish's vile end, convinced me not to consider that option. *The death of a Betta can take weeks*, Google told me. *Slow, agonizing weeks.* I could see that already. *Do your fish a favor*, one article advised. *Put him out of his misery.* Suggestions included placing my fish on a hard surface, like a cement porch or a tile floor, and stomping fast and hard. Or placing the fish on a cutting board and chopping off his head. Ellis had a cleaver. Maybe I could ask him to do the honors. Nah, I'd have to do this myself, and now, while I had the nerve. I decided on solution number three: pour a jigger of vodka in the fish bowl; place the fish in a zipper bag; put the bag in the freezer. The posting assured me I would be carrying out a grand act of kindness, and, as an hour passed, I could believe the truth of it.

I took the first shot myself. When I administered David's, the alcohol seemed to bring him back to life. Or, oh God, it was running through him like fire. I gave us both another helping. He wasn't moving like the old days, but the next dose straightened him and he floated right side up. Straight away, I brought out the net and scooped David into the bag. I topped him off with extra vodka, but I didn't feel kind, not by a longshot. By the time I propped him between Dreamsicles and a slab of wild salmon, David and I were both pretty well embalmed. I fell into bed and passed out.

Next morning, when I went for my multigrain waffle, the sight of my small dead fish wounded me. A fish is not a dog. Not even a cat. Don't think that I don't understand that. But through that cruelest month, David had been a bright spark in my kitchen. He would be missed.

I picked him up and looked him over. Although his good eye was wide open and perfectly clear, the ice that encased him had turned pale yellow and mealy. What next? I wasn't about to flush him after I'd done what I had to avoid it. The garbage disposal was out of the question.

That evening, I poured potting soil two fingers deep into the fish bowl. I lifted David out of the bag by his tail and placed him, unthawed, in the center, all his hearts and marbles around him. In went more dirt, a slip of rosemary on top. I set the bowl on the table beneath my long window and drew up the blinds to let in the view: by day, the sky outside spreads itself into an endless lake; by night, it swims with stars.

The Truth About "The Lead Plates at the Romm Press": A Lecture by Abraham Sutzkever

Alison Morse

Second Prize
Short Story

"Arrayed at night, like fingers stretched through bars
To clutch the lit air of freedom,
We made for the press plates, to seize
The lead plates at the Romm printing works.
We were dreamers, we had to be soldiers,
And melt down, for our bullets, the spirit of the lead."[1]

Yes, I wrote those words in 1943. Now, if I'm to understand you correctly, more than sixty years later, you want to know if I, Abraham Sutzkever, was actually telling the truth? Did the Jewish underground in Vilna really melt lead type from the Romm Press into bullets, or did I simply make the whole thing up just to write a poem? It tickles me that you're still interested. I've heard scholars are still giving lectures and seminars on the subject; they hold debates about Sutzkever and his Romm Press poem in chat rooms and blogs, discussions that have lasted for years. If I printed out all the arguments and laid them end to end, they'd be longer than the Vilna sewers. Of course, Holocaust scholars make a living out of questions like this. "There's no way Sutzkever and those partisans melted the Romm Press letters into bullets. Ghetto furnaces couldn't generate enough heat to keep people warm, let alone melt lead printing plates." I know it's always been an academic's job to (pardon the cliché) miss the forest for the trees. What I love are the rebuttals. One imaginative blogger insists: "The partisans didn't need any more heat to melt lead than they had to cook cholent every Sabbath." I wait to see a chat room claim that you can melt lead plates with the farts you get after eating cholent. But I'm digressing. You say you want the truth? Let me tell you a story.

* * *

When I was a boy, I watched my older sister skip the fourth year of school, then the fifth and sixth. Her brown eyes were glazed from sitting up nights memorizing—in their original Russian— Pushkin, Lermontov, even Blok—not just our own Yiddish poets. I'd pass her room on the way to bed and would see her black braids curtaining whatever book she was ingesting. I wanted to pull one of those night colored ropes just to get her attention.

At eleven—just three years older than me—she wrote her first verse in Russian. "Genius" is what the teachers and my mother called my sister of the long black braids, ends likes pen nibs, skin as pale as the pages she read. She wrote in a fever in our little hut in Vilna, by candlelight, her braids lying dangerously close to the dripping wax.

"What are you doing?" I asked her.

"I'm dancing."

"It must be a very bad dance."

She giggled and threw a balled-up piece of paper at me. Her laugh was a melody in B Minor.

Our father was already dead. One night, while fiddling the old song "Thou, Thou Thou," his violin began to shake. Then he collapsed on top of me. I was seven, the family baby with arms too weak to catch him. Within seconds, his white skin turned blue. I could no longer hear his breath.

My sister and I inherited Father's white skin.

Sometime after her thirteenth birthday, my sister began to turn purple: first her toes and fingertips then her arms and legs, as if ink had seeped underneath her skin. She lay in bed shivering, sweating, stiff, but did not complain; only said the candle flame was too bright.

One night I woke up to loud thuds against the wall that separated my sister from me. It was the sound of her bed frame banging into the wall while invisible hands gripped her in a convulsive partner dance. "Brain fever," is what my mother whispered to our aunt. The doctor said "Meningitis." My older sister swelled. She could no longer answer when I asked how she was doing; she had lost her ability to hear our world. But she did sound out mysterious words as if she were conversing with someone I couldn't see and followed this phantom's spasmodic lead with the jerk of an arm or leg.

On a warm summer morning, while sitting alone with my sister, she looked at me and opened her mouth as if to speak. Then she turned into a ribbon of ink that flew out the window on a traveling breeze. I know this because I saw the word *eternal* purpled on the window above her bed.

As soon as this happened, I ran out to the bank of the Viliya River and wrote the word *eternal* in the sand.

You look at me incredulously; but it's true. In the sand I wrote my first poem. Once I started writing I couldn't stop. Not even when I was hiding from the Germans in the chimney of the house I shared with my wife Freydke, could I put down my pen.

Up until then we were 60,000, we Jews of Vilna. Anti-communist intellectuals didn't have it so good, but, in general, the Lithuanians and Russians left us alone to live our lives. Writing was easy. My poetry sang rhymed melodies to a moment's purple shimmer—which drove my socialist, communist, Bundist writer-comrades crazy.

"Avram," they used to nag. "How is it you stick your head in the sand when all of Eastern Europe is in a tumult. Your lack of political engagement is obscene."

But I didn't care. Let the Russians and Germans argue over who got what in Eastern Europe; I was preoccupied with the snow white breath of the shooting star I saw the night before.

That is, until 1941.

Under the summer solstice sun, the Nazis marched into Vilna to grab up every able-bodied Jewish man they could find. Just like that, a pack of thugs could drag you to a work camp to cut peat bricks for the Germans; or you could end up in Lukiszki prison then the forest, never to be heard from again. Sometimes you weren't grabbed; you were simply the target of a rifle butt or a bullet while you were waiting in line to buy bread.

I was young and able-bodied, fearful of being taken. For six weeks I hid in the chimney of our house battling something unspeakable that was trying to strangle the musical rhymes of my poetry. Where was the beauty in lines that rhymed smoke with choke, game with lame, fresh with flesh, fall with all? Very quickly, my rhymes began to break down. Soon I was writing stanzas with no rhymes at all; lines that ended with spectacle, curse, death, Roman, pain, pox, grave, mercy. I wanted to erase those dark moments inside the bricks, not sing them. I wanted to erase myself for leaving Freydke all alone.

At the first sign of a lull in the Nazi's pursuit of young men, I left the chimney, only to watch—utterly helpless—the grabbing of everything we owned: our warm coats, our boots, our furniture, our air.

The Nazis shoved us, we 15,000 surviving Jews, into seven walled-in city blocks and forced us to guard each other day and night; Jewish rifles pointed at Jewish heads. The other 45,000? We were taken to pits in the forest and told to sit on the edge. Then shot.

And the Germans grabbed our words. Illuminated Torahs, Talmuds, Haggadahs and books by our best Yiddish authors: Peretz, Mendele, Sholem Aleichem, Perl; Yiddish dictionaries; whole libraries from other cities were treated like wood chips to be burned or pulped.

The pages that held my chimney verses waved like little white flags. The poems on them bleated *surrender*, surrender to each new Nazi order: to become a working slave, to starve on potato peels, to walk numbly down the street past the dead bodies of neighbors, to give up friends to the police in the hope that I would be spared.

Inside the ghetto hospital Freydke gave birth to a boy, an illegal act—Jews were forbidden to have offspring. A soldier grabbed him as soon as he cried and fed him poison. I was not allowed to be by her side, but Freydke held a poem of mine in her fist the entire time. I hated that poem. It couldn't save my family. I needed to transform my passive lines on paper into life-saving, life avenging bullets.

I joined the United Partisan Organization. A tiny group of us smuggled guns in and out of the ghetto, learned to make bombs out of light bulbs filled with gas, hid in a cellar and practiced aiming a pistol at the imaginary necks of Nazi soldiers.

And I joined the Paper Brigade: Jews who worked for the Rosenberg Bureau gathering material for a new collection: "the science of Jewry without Jews." On my job I could grab back our books and manuscripts, our language. Our German supervisors couldn't read Hebrew or Yiddish; we had to tell them what was important enough to ship to Germany and what could be sent to the paper mill. At the end of a workday I carried a book in my coat back to the ghetto, a collection of Sholem Aleichem short stories, or maybe one of Theodor Herzl's diaries, and swore I was going to burn it to heat my home. So did Freydke. The trick worked over and over until we had suitcases full of Talmuds, Torahs, Yiddish history texts, journals, poetry, novels, letters that we hid in a secret place beneath the basement. They had taken our boy; we would not let them take our language.

The Romm Press plates were another matter. Neither of us could carry the heavy lead printing plates in our coats. What were we to do with the weight of all those years the press spent gathering commentary, ancient and modern, and proofreading every letter, space and line for their Vilna Talmud? How could we preserve the gleaming columns of the Talmud's frontispiece illustration or the press's dancing-seriffed Vilna font? When you melt something into something else, does it lose its essence?

When orders came from Hitler to liquidate the Vilna ghetto, most of my neighbors surrendered to the boxcars that transported them to the next work camp and their deaths.

Freydke and I took a different path. Into the sewer pipes underneath Vilna we crept, following our Jewish partisan comrades through the city's wastewater, where swollen bodies of dead Jews floated, blocking our passage. We had to move them to get to where we were going: into the Narocz forest to join the Russian Communist partisan resistance forces. We were fighters, not martyrs, immersed in a mikvah of human waste.

But as soon as we reached the forest camp, Russian commanders ordered us to give up our weapons. Our job, as Jews, was to carry the wounded and sick past German soldiers through swamps, snow, fields of frozen bodies. We were starving and covered with shit. How could we refuse?

The purple evening I dragged my first soldier onto a stretcher, his leg split open by shrapnel, I remembered the night my father's heart seized. He toppled into my seven-year old arms that were too thin to keep us both from landing on the floor. Into my ear he whispered: "That's right. Try bearing life's weight now, so your hands can get used to holding it later." Then he died.

Ladies and gentlemen, I only write what I believe is true. I made words into bullets to save my wife and me and the memory of our son. In the ghetto, I'd given handwritten copies of my poems to partisans who brought them to Moscow. The anti-Nazi Lithuanian president, exiled in Moscow, was a poet too. He ordered a rescue plane to bring us out of the forest, away from German territory. But to get to the plane, Freydke and I had to walk along a railroad track in an open field, mines to the left and right of us, mines along the tracks. I led the way, chanting each line out loud, walking to the rhythm of my poems. Freydke followed my footsteps exactly. Our dark bodies wrote living Yiddish words in the snow.

And if you really want to know, the last poem that I recited, the one that finally got us from the field to the frozen lake where the rescue plane awaited, I am sure was this:

"We were dreamers," step,
"we had to be soldiers," step,
"And melt down," step,
"for our bullets," step,
"the spirit of the lead," step.[2]

---

[1] from "The Lead Plates at the Romm Press," Abraham Sutzkever, translated by Neal Kozodoy.

[2] Ibid.

Super Nova

Gary Powell

Honorable
Mention
Short Story

By the time I drag home from track practice my folks have already eaten, leaving a plate out for me. Like most evenings, the old man is into his third CC and Seven, reading the newspaper, and my mom has her hair up in rollers, watching some sitcom with Lucy and Ethel. This evening's no different, except Jerry Schumacher is on the sofa chatting with my old man. I already knew Jerry was here because I saw his car out front when Coach Kelly dropped me off—that '68 Super Nova Jerry went into debt for last summer.

He's telling the old man he's put in new headers and a Positraction rear end. He's saying he took down Jim Wiedemeier's Mustang out on Cable Line Road last Saturday night. The old man's eating it up, because he likes fast cars. He likes Jerry, too, even though Jerry dropped out of school last year and has gone about as far in life as he's going to go. He builds floors at Nomad RV, sticking every penny into that Super Nova.

"Hey, Mikey." Jerry stands when he notices me in the archway. He used to run track, too, but he looks like a factory-guy now, not a runner. He's broad across the shoulders, beer-thick around the waist, straight from work in his grimy jeans, flannel shirt, and Carhartt vest. Come October, he'll turn eighteen. This time next year he'll likely be crawling through rice paddies, just trying to stay alive.

"This past weekend, he put in a new tranny and Hurst shifter all by himself," my old man says.

Jerry grins. "Coulda' used your help."

I'd gone for long runs Saturday and Sunday, gutting it out in sleet both days, my first meet coming up in two weeks. "You shoulda' said something."

"Maybe you shoulda' asked," my old man says. Jerry's old

man died of a heart attack last year, which was the reason Jerry gave for dropping out of school and going to work.

My mom looks up from her magazine. "There's pot roast and mashed potatoes under the tin-foil."

I'm never hungry after practice, but that meat and potatoes won't look any better later on, so I pour myself a glass of milk and sit down at the table. Jerry sits down with me, my old man not far behind. He fetches Jerry a beer from the refrigerator.

"How's your mom?" he asks.

Jerry reaches into his shirt pocket, digs out a pack of Winstons, and lights up. "Day to day."

My old man chews the ice in his drink. "Your dad was a good man. Steady, real steady."

"What I heard."

My old man nudges my arm. "Jerry wants to take you for a ride."

That Super Nova has a 300 horsepower 350 small-block engine under the hood. I know what kind of ride we're in for. I inhale dinner and drain my glass. I should stretch and hit the weights in the basement. I should do my homework. I carry my plate to the sink, scrape, and rinse off.

"I appreciate that," my mom sings out.

"All right, let's go." I'm still dressed in sweats and stocking cap, still sticky and salty from the track.

Jerry and my old man share a laugh about something I don't catch. "Give a man a chance to finish his beer," my old man says.

I've read that an actual supernova is an exploding star, an act of self-destruction, beautiful and terrible to behold, matter turning to energy at the speed of light. Jerry's Super Nova is a Chevy II family car re-invented as a street racer. The factory cream has been re-painted a bolder, brighter yellow. Custom black pin-striping accents the downward slope of the hood and trunk. He's jazzed up the look with chrome wheels and hood locks. The black Naugahyde interior smells like cigarettes and after-shave. We slide inside and he fires her up, a rumble and a shudder.

"Try it," he says.

I cup the Hurst shifter in my palm. It fits like a cue-ball, smooth and round, a scary power underneath. Four hundred dollars, one week's piece-work pay, just for the shifter.

We creep out of the drive way, custom wide tires crunching on gravel. It's April, but snow still lies in drifts along the road. Winter lingers long here, and we're still expecting one final snow, deep and wet off of Lake Michigan. We know it's coming, but that last one surprises every year. About the time you plant corn, take the chains off your tires, or start thinking about baseball, here it comes.

Once he's on pavement, Jerry pops the clutch and lays half a mile of rubber. I know my old man's at the door listening for that sick squeal.

We drive down Mishawaka Avenue, then turn left on Benham headed into town. Jerry says his work isn't so bad. It's all the dumbasses he has to put up with. Once a week, someone loses a finger to a saw blade. Two guys got into a fight the week before last and one of them shot the other in the throat with a nail gun. Then there's all the pussy he's getting. Not just high school girls, but older women, married women and divorcees he meets at the factory. One look at his Super Nova and they cream their jeans.

Jerry flicks a butt out the window and asks what's new.

I say not much, but the truth is I'm running a four and a quarter mile, a time that could take me through Sectionals and Regionals and all the way to State. Coach Kelly's talking college. He's talking scholarship and student deferment from the draft

Jerry turns off Benham onto Hively and pulls up in front of Chip LeMaster's house. Chip and Randy Miller are in the garage, under the hood of Chip's black on black '62 Impala. They're half-way though a case of Bud, beery and red-faced despite the cold. Chip quarterbacked and Randy played tailback on a team that won State last year. Off-season, Coach Kelly made them run track and cross country, but there's no off-season once you're out of school.

"It's Spin and Marty," LeMaster says.

"The Bobbsey Twins," Miller says.

I can see Jerry wants these guys for his friends, football stars, the kind of guys people talk about for years. Maybe it's an even trade, because they want him for his car and what he knows about cars. Even if I win State, no one remembers a runner.

LeMaster's a big guy, blonde haired and barrel-chested, rugged and tough for a quarterback. He walked on at Ball State, but didn't last. Now, he's working construction, living at home. Miller's tall and lean, a natural born runner if it wasn't for his blown-out knee. Not all that bright, they held him back twice. He'd already be in 'Nam except that knee bought him a 4-F. He pumps gas at Phillips 66 on north Main.

"You guys comin' or what?" Jerry asks.

"Fixin' this piece a shit," Miller says, dark, curly hair falling into darker eyes. Everyone knows his old man did time down state.

Jerry leans in, fingers the carburetor, adjusts a hose. He's got a knack. "That valve's stuck. You ever change the oil?"

LeMaster shines a hand-held light. "Get outta' here."

"Clean that carburetor, be good as new."

Miller wipes his hands on a greasy rag, looks me over with those eyes. "How they hangin', Runner?"

"You know."

"Goin' to State?"

"Maybe."

"Winnin' State?"

"Maybe."

LeMaster closes the hood. "Those niggers'll run you in the ground."

I've heard it before, how us white boys can't hang with the blacks. Miller grins. He's lost a tooth since I saw him last. "Let 'em out fast, then reel 'em in."

"That how you did it?" Jerry asks.

"I left 'em in the dust. I didn't look back."

LeMaster hands out beers all around. "C'mon. Enough bullshit. Let's find some ass."

Jerry starts for his Super Nova. "Now you're talkin'."

According to the City Council, Elkhart is the RV capital of the world, one millionaire for every thousand people. But my old man says there's rich and then there's hillbilly rich, and we've got more than our share of hillbillies come north looking for work. Add them to the blacks and Dagos and Polacks already here, and it can get rough.

The roughest part, aside from the factories, is The Drag. Come summer, Main Street's bumper to bumper from the train tracks to the turn-around, guys in muscle cars, chicks in halter tops. The hotter it gets, the more fights there are. Beat some guy off his mark, a fight breaks out. Look at some guy's girl wrong, a fight breaks out. No one backs down, because once you back down you're done on The Drag. There's no shame in taking a beating. There's no guilt in delivering one. But no one backs down.

One night here can change a life, same as a touchdown pass thrown in desperation or a four-minute mile can change a life, same as a blown-out knee or an old man dying before his time can change a life. We cruise past Azar's and McDonald's and the sign on north Main that reminds us and the rest of the world of who we are—Elkhart, the City with a Heart.

George Fonte's here in his '58 Edsel. Wild Man Roy Burgess has the top down on his '63 'Vette. They eye us at the stoplights, revving engines and marking territory. A few more old guys, veterans of the cruising wars, gather in the Post Office parking lot, shooting a cold breeze, pissing in a prairie wind. Missing tonight is the younger crowd you see on weekends, the Major brothers from Jimtown, the Cantrells from Edwardsburg. Missing, too, are the girls in halter tops and short-shorts, pretending they're not interested. Middle of the week, dirty snow piled in corners, the girls are at home, painting their nails, curling their hair in rollers big as Coke cans.

We take several laps, train tracks to the turn-around, searching for a spark, but with every lap expectations fade. Resignation sets in and gives way to a despair that fogs the windows no less than our breath. Anyone can see that other than a knifing on Harrison or a shooting behind the Cozy Corner, nothing's going down tonight.

"Slow," Jerry says.

"Slow as molasses," LeMaster agrees.

I'm in back with Miller. His head rests on the seat, eyes closed.

He keeps his bad right leg stretched straight. "Let's ditch this scene," he says. "See what this pussy-wagon can do in the quarter mile." Jerry doesn't like it. "Give me a break. I'm haulin' three guys." LeMaster punches him on the shoulder. "C'mon, take her out to Cable Line. Show us what she's got."

Jerry might not like running the quarter mile with all this extra weight, but he's not saying no to LeMaster and Miller. One more lap, and then we head out of town, out to the back roads, to see what Jerry's Super Nova's really got.

I used to date this girl, Suzie Vance, lived next to the railroad tracks. One night we watched that Hitchcock movie, "Psycho" and made out on her parents' sofa until after midnight, passing trains shaking the house. I drove home in my old man's Ford Falcon, three-speed on the column. Corner of Cable Line and Prairie, I swear a man stood up out of the ditch and waved at me. Already jumpy from the movie, I lost the engine when I came off the line. Jimmy-legged, I got her going again, then fish-tailed onto the shoulder and nearly rolled into the ditch.

The Ghost of Cable Line they call that tree looks like a dead man waving. He's out on moonlit summer nights, corn higher than your head, cow manure ripe in your nostrils. Tonight, there's none of that. Snow skitters across moonless fields picked clean last fall. Cows snuggle for warmth in their barns. No one else is out, no street lights shine. Driving here's like driving through a tunnel carved by headlights.

We make the run from Oakland to Harding Road. Guys, long before us, have marked the quarter miles, more than a few with their blood. Jerry opens her up, that big engine whining. He shows us where he left Wiedemeier's Mustang in the dust. We swing past the high school and take another run. It's then LeMaster sees the twin beams behind us.

"Who ya' figure?" Jerry asks.

"Don't recognize him," LeMaster says.

Miller glances over his shoulder. "He's gainin'."

Jerry sneers. "Watch this."

He punches the accelerator and I feel a force like a heavy

hand push into my chest. When I manage a look, the twin beams are even closer.

"No way," Jerry says.

Miller rests a hand on Jerry's shoulder, his lips close enough to kiss Jerry's cheek. "Guess it ain't Wiedemeir's Mustang."

Jerry cuts him a look in the rearview.

"Slow down, slow down," LeMaster says.

Jerry downshifts and rolls through the stop sign at County Road 11.

"Fuckin' Ford Galaxy," Miller says.

"Punch it," LeMaster says.

Jerry hits the gas again, flattening us to our seats. The Galaxy's lights dim, then brighten.

"He can't do that," Jerry says.

"Hell he can't." Miller's enjoying this, seeing Jerry squirm.

"Turn up there," LeMaster tells him.

Jerry wheels into the horseshoe drive at Stickel's farm. We skid sideways, cinders flying. Jerry holds tight and brings the Super Nova around, shooting past the Galaxy headed the other way on the Cable Line Road.

We can't believe it when the Galaxy makes an even tighter turn. Coming up on the Ghost Tree, he crawls up our tail pipe. When Jerry slows, the guy's headlights flash.

LeMaster rolls his window down, leans through, and flips the driver the bird with both hands. Headlights flash on and off, on and off.

"Pull over at the church," Miller says. "Find out who this is."

"I don't know," Jerry says.

"Pull over," LeMaster says. "It's four of us to one of him."

Mt. Pleasant church on Prairie, Jerry pulls into the parking lot, slows to a stop. Across the way, a guy climbs out of the Galaxy. He's a man, old enough for a wife and family, a steady job. LeMaster and Miller are ahead of Jerry and me.

"Hey," LeMaster says.

The guy's flashlight is on us. "What're you boys up to?"

Miller steps forward. "Who's askin'?"

"Stop right there." The guy says he's an off-duty cop, says he needs to detain us.

Jerry looks at me, then the guy. "What'd we do? We didn't do anything."

"Speeding, reckless driving, running a stop sign. Let me see your license, son."

"You did it, too," LeMaster says. "No one's hurt. What's the problem?"

"The problem is you broke the law."

"We didn't know you was a cop," Jerry says. "You didn't light us up."

"I'm off-duty."

"The fuck's that mean?" Miller says. "If you're off-duty, why aren't you home?"

"Give me your keys and your license," the guy tells Jerry, "or I'll throw in resisting arrest."

Jerry wraps his arms around his chest. "Let's see your badge."

"It's in the car. Like I said, I'm off-duty."

LeMaster edges closer "He's no cop."

The guy holds his ground. "Look, you don't want more trouble than you're already in."

"He's just some guy jackin' us," Miller says.

"I've got a radio. I've already called for back-up."

"Yeah, right." Miller takes two steps and the guy sets himself, maybe thinking he's a man against a boy, not knowing Miller grew up fighting his old man for everything he ever got.

But it's LeMaster on the guy first, fast and hard, a left to his midsection, a right to his jaw. The guy sags to his knees. When he looks up, blood, thick and dark as syrup, drips from his nose to the pavement. He wipes it with his sleeve. "Dumb-ass. I told you I called for back-up."

In the distance, sirens wail. Maybe those sirens belong to us, maybe not. Maybe they belong to an accident on Highway 19 or a robbery at a liquor store. Things are happening fast, but not so fast we couldn't call time out, couldn't call a false start.

Then Miller wades in and delivers another blow to the guy's face. When the guy topples, Miller kicks him three, four times, his good leg doing the damage. This is no broken-field run with feints and missed tackles, with swiveling hips and Heisman poses.

This is a dive over the middle, a lowered shoulder, a straight-arm to the throat.

LeMaster pulls him off. "Easy, Randy, easy."

Miller bellows into the night. "Who's the dumb-ass, now?"

I can make out two sirens, one from each direction on Cable Line Road. The guy Miller kicked doesn't move. His head lies at an odd angle from his shoulder.

A hot, nauseous rush clamps my throat shut.

"Where you going?" Jerry asks.

The highlights reel shows me backing away. The nightly news clip shows this Marine retreating in the face of enemy fire.

"Mikey, stop. Where you goin'?" Jerry's voice is high-pitched, a little kid's voice.

LeMaster's got him by the arm. "Get in the car."

"Where's he goin'?"

"C'mon. Let's roll," Miller says.

I edge closer to the road.

"What about Mikey?"

Miller pushes Jerry hard. "Get in the fuckin' car, now."

LeMaster waves me off. "Go on. Get outta' here."

"Go, Runner," Miller says. "Don't look back."

I set off north across the fields, passing close enough to the Ghost Tree to slap the man's hand. It's no more than three miles to my house. It's dark and I can't see, but that's in my favor because neither can they. I hear car doors slam, hear the roar of that Super Nova and sirens closing in. We all know, the 350 Nova's no match for a 427 Galaxy.

I put my head down and break through the soreness and stiffness. After the first half mile I find my pace. I sail over broken corn stalks and frozen ruts, the only light that of a few distant stars shining through the breaking clouds. I wonder what my old man will say when he reads about this in tomorrow's paper.

CREATIVE NONFICTION

Judged by Tracy Crow

First Prize: Leslie Tucker of Landrum, SC
for "Lies That Bind"

Second Prize: Sandell Morse of York, ME
for "The Groves"

Honorable Mention: Hannah Karena Jones of Langhorne, PA
for "What to Expect While Grieving for Your Father"

2012
PRESS 53
OPEN AWARDS

Finalists:

Sandy Barnett-Ebner of Danville, CA for "The Clothes I Was Wearing"

Betty Jo Goddard of Anchor Point, AK for "Schism"

Judith Hertog of Norwich, VA for "The Red and the Black"

Beverly Jackson of Naples, FL for "Swan Song"

Suzanne Kamata of Tokumei, Japan for "Lilia's World"

Daniel B. Meltzer of New York, NY for "Witchcraft"

Lies That Bind

Leslie Tucker

First Prize
Creative
Nonfiction

At high school parties I danced all the fast dances, some by myself, sweat streaming beneath my clothing, sometimes soaking my spiral-stitched Maidenform. I guzzled Stroh's and made out with boys for arbitrary reasons, like how fast they could conjugate French verbs in falsetto, or solve quadratic equations without checking the answers at the back of the book, or especially, if they had small tight asses and sneered like Mick Jagger. I compared the textures of their tongues but dated the ones who let me drive their cars. Inspired at stoplights on Woodward, I gunned the muscular engines of a GTO, a Plymouth Barracuda, even a Mustang like the one in *Goldfinger*.

I'm pretty sure my fascination with the physical began on a sweltering July day when I was four years old and overwhelmed by the visceral thrill of grainy glop squishing through my bare toes. I'd flooded my brother's sandbox with the garden hose and created a cake batter of golden mud that rose up to the tiny triangular seats in each corner. I stepped in, swirled the cool, knee-deep muck with my skinny little hands and squealed. By age nine I was bumping up and down over curbs with my 24 inch Schwinn, relishing the brain buzz of clunking molars, and by junior high I raced against myself around the perimeter of the gym, deliriously dizzy with speed while other girls practiced cheerleading.

Sure, it's clear now that my nascent physical cravings were instinctual, and that my unruly behavior blasted Mother's paradigm for a daughter to smithereens and enlarged the emotional morass between us as years passed. Sadly for her, the good-girl-daughter Mother believed she'd been raising never showed up, and by sixteen, that girl figured she was lost and let it rip.

But I'd learned to lie to her long before that.

* * *

As a rambunctious little girl, lying never occurred to me when Mother asked how I got grass stains on my starched pink playsuit. "Turning somersaults with Janie," I giggled, and out came the hand-painted hairbrush, spankings being common discipline in the 1950s. Later that summer, she caught Janie and me peeing under an enormous hemlock that seemed like Red Riding Hood's woods, and again, out popped the hairbrush. That particular spanking occurred in our back yard, within earshot of porch-sitting neighbors who gaped as Mother shrieked, "You've humiliated me. Aren't you ashamed?" Shame? Humiliation? I hadn't a clue, but her tight-lipped red face and the welts on my legs? Those, I understood. From then on, if I peed outdoors I made sure it was further from home.

Mother and I were compulsive liars with each other and it was not until the last four days of her life that I examined how and why our pattern of lies developed. She was moaning in her hospital bed, morphine dripping fast, and I sweated like swine in the overheated room, face sticking to a purple vinyl chair pulled up next to her. I slumped and dozed in the darkness, haunted by our lifetime of deceit and wondered when I'd become aware that our personal truths opposed each other: that mine were rooted in the physical, hers, embedded in propriety. When had it become easy for me to lie to her and when did our estrangement develop into my frenzied rebellion? Speculating on the answers to those questions seemed simple, but it has never been simple to understand who she really was. What was it that thrilled her? Were she and I really so different?

Mother was beautiful and bright light smart, had graduated 2nd in her class from a prestigious Detroit high school at age sixteen. She'd yearned for a college education, told me she'd been sickened with disappointment in her parents who barely kept their large family fed during the Great Depression of the 1930s. When she'd pleaded with her father about going to college, he'd responded: So go.

This was Mother's story, as she told and retold it, all emphasis on the ever-enduring moment when the stellar accomplishments of her young life were dismissed by the hunched shoulders and upturned palms of a failed old man. It would be forty years before I learned, by accident, that Mother had omitted important elements of the story.

Mother worked two jobs while attending college at night but never graduated because she met Dad at the Fairmont Creamery soda fountain where she scooped ice cream on weekends. He wandered in after the service at the gothic Methodist fortress across Woodward and she discarded her Catholicism on the spot. She lit up a Revlon red smile, plopped an extra scoop of vanilla into his Vernor's float and cut the deal of her lifetime. From that day forward she saved every shred of herself for him. She waited while he finished law school, went to War, collected evidence for a year after the war and prosecuted war crimes at Nuremburg. She told anyone who would listen that post war life with her beloved had been a dream until her colicky daughter was born eleven months after his return.

Mother told anyone who asked that she was English. Once, when bridge club was held at our home, her close friend, Cass, daughter of a prominent Detroit doctor, pressed Mother for information about her lineage, specifically which branch of the Dales she was from. Mother hesitated a second. "Oh dear, there are so many of us in Detroit, not to mention Michigan and Ohio. I've never paid enough attention to know. Anyway, what are you reading these days, Cass?" And before Cass could answer, Mother said she was rereading *Jane Eyre*, that her love of English Literature, the Bronte sisters in particular, was bred into her bones. Whenever I brought forms home from school requiring "Mother's Maiden Name," she filled in "Dale."

Mother's story satisfied me until an autumn day in third grade when my class was assigned a family tree project. We were challenged to be junior detectives, to discover which countries both sets of our grand parents came from, to write their names on tiny flags and stick them on the limbs of construction paper trees. Dad's parents, my Nana and Grandpa, were intimate regulars in my life, and suddenly I was excited, wondering if there might be another pair of storytellers who sang and held my hands as we strolled to the neighborhood bakery.

I bolted home from school and rushed in the back door, breathless. "Mrs. Woodworth says we all have two sets of grandparents. Where are my other ones?" Mother's face puckered up sideways and the can opener she was twisting clunked down onto the floor.

"My parents have been dead for decades."

"Did they die in the War? Did they come from far away? Mrs. Woodworth says lots of kids have grandparents that came to America from far away and we can find the countries on the map."

A purplish shade of red spread up Mother's neck onto her face, nearly as dark as the beets splattered on the counter from the half-opened can. Her chin jutted forward and the cords in her neck popped out as she enunciated.

"Long ago, everyone came from far away, but we are all Americans now."

"But what were their names?"

"Whose names?"

"My other Nana and Grandpa's...you know, your parents..."

"Of course I know. Zofia and Jozef."

I'd never heard names like those. I asked Mother to spell them, said the only Z-word I knew was "zebra," and that zebras lived in Africa, far away. She flushed. I'd gotten a rise out of her but wasn't afraid, somehow knew I'd caught her off guard.

Maybe I sensed the murky drama that would play out between us, or was just being troublesome and perfecting the art of pushing her emotional buttons. I brought up the family tree project at dinner and asked Dad, "Did you know my other Grandpa and Grandma before they died?" He stayed silent, a surprised grimace on his face as he turned to catch Mother's eye. She refused to look at him, glowered at me and defamed my teacher.

"Mrs. Woodworth assigned this project? Any woman who

would be caught dead in those stumpy heeled oxfords can't be very smart."

It would be forty years before I learned the truth, that Mother had changed her name, legally, to Dale, eight weeks before she married Dad in 1942.

I recognize now that my lying began soon after I learned to spell the name Zofia, with the Z. It was simple. I did it the same way I'd been taught to cross a busy street. Before opening my mouth, I stopped, looked at Mother's face, listened to her tone of voice and observed the cords in her neck. When I gashed my chin, flipping over the handlebars on my bike while jumping a curb, I automatically lied, said I'd stumbled on the playground. I think I lied solely to her as I grew up, and that my awkward blurting of dramatic truth to most everyone else became an embarrassing personality trademark as I came of age.

By the time I suspected Mother was lying about her family background we were well entrenched in Birmingham, an upper middle class suburb northwest of Detroit. In our neighborhood, Mother may well have been the only woman whose father hadn't bought her cashmere sweaters and paid her way through college, or at least supported her until she landed an appropriate husband. I remember her close friends in their later years, their Anglo-Saxon names, their sorority talk, their husbands' letter sweaters wrapped in yellowed tissue, symbolic old lady treasure in assisted living apartments. It's easy to imagine how ill at ease Mother must have felt in her own life. The women surrounding her had lived the life she'd wanted, and although she ended up on the same socio-economic planet, she was an alien there. Every move she made was calculated, had to be proper, perfect from all angles of observation. And of course, so did I.

How exhausting it must have been for Mother to strive for social prestige and acceptance with every breath, to maintain the perfect lady act on the stage of her life. Her ever-present strand of pearls, the lacquered hairdo, that rail straight posture with legs crossed only at the ankle.

Her harsh self-judgment, I recognize now, all these years later, must have translated into her signature litanies on others. Didn't Cass realize her short hair looked downright mannish on such a tall woman, and why did Dee slop around the neighborhood in those flat-heeled shoes? Why ever would fat Katherine stand on her porch bellowing like a fish wife for her boys to come home instead of establishing the time in advance? And what possessed Clarence Morgan to buy a second car for his wife if it had to be a used one with a rusted door panel? But she let their children go barefooted, so it figured.

Mother's favorite subject was identifying bad girls and good girls and her ideas dripped into my ear like midsummer night's poison long before I understood what bad might mean. Or how much I liked it. Sadly, before I could grasp what made a girl bad, I'd deduced that no matter how she lectured or dressed me up, I had plenty of bad girl traits and was comfortable with them.

I was boisterous, ran stupid fast and bumped into trees sometimes, legs trembling as I collapsed on the ground. I tore around on my bike, whooped like the boys, and as Mother put it, had too much energy for my own good. I came home with crud on my clothes, tracked mud onto sparkling white linoleum without thinking and easily internalized the stigma of being "bad" when I was punished.

I was fearless, and learned to be shameless.

At what age do we begin to construct our adult selves, our self-images? And what developmental milestones help us decide who we will be? For me, an important milestone was at age eight, in second grade, when I hung by my knees from the jungle bars at recess, blithely showing droopy cotton underpants. The gathered skirt of my starched dress flopped down over my head and although other girls screeched and boys howled, I wasn't embarrassed. I imagined myself in a tent, or hiding behind the heavy silk drapes in our living room. My scrawny knees gripped the bar, blood rushed to my head and I swung back and forth, arms swinging like chimpanzees I'd seen at the zoo. Mother's manicured hand trembled later that day, after she'd been summoned to the principal's office. She shut the door on her way out, saw me waiting on the little chair and whispered through gritted teeth.

"Only bad girls show their underpants."

"But how can I hang by my knees?"

"Good girls don't hang by their knees."

I loved hanging upside down, feeling the breeze on my bare belly button.

When do good girls turn into bad ones and does the transformation sync up with enjoying physical sensations and the aura of danger surrounding those sensations? Some of us learn early that we hunger for speed, for wind blasting our faces and rippling our hair. We're exhilarated by racing on young legs, flying along no-handed on our bicycles, and later, driving too fast. For me, early physical thrills evolved into a craving for more advanced sensations, and the transfiguration from good to so-called bad had already occurred by the time I discovered I was aroused and enjoyed what boys wanted to do. Learning that I could direct their performance and radically improve the excitement was a stunning breakthrough for a teenaged girl in the mid-1960s. As I've aged, the physical ecstasy of my life, from sexual experiences to bungee jumping and sky diving, is indelibly imprinted, an invisible tattoo of primitive, personal truth that dazzles my sixty-four-year-old mind.

Today's concept of children as individual beings wasn't readily embraced in our family's social circle in the 1950s, when children's behavior was representative of a woman's mothering skill and established her primal value. With one exception, all the women in the neighborhood where our family lived considered home making and mothering a full-time job, a privileged position earned by those who'd waited for men to come home from World War II and occupy their rightful places as heads of households.

My parents felt fortunate that Dad had survived gruesome combat, returned without injuries, and was able to earn enough for our family to be comfortable. In Mother's world of the 1950s, as she often told me, a woman's worth was determined by three factors: Her beauty, her grooming, and most important, her children's behavior. The equation was simple: Sassy child equaled deficient mother.

And I was a sassy child, then a belligerent, rebellious teenager. Yes, a common mother-daughter story, except that most mothers and daughters I've known fought about the truth, or at least what they perceived to be the truth. My mother and I lied, knew we were lying, and then fought about the lies we told each other. I don't believe our lies were premeditated, or that we even wanted to tell them. I lied because Mother disapproved of what I believed in, of what I wanted. She lied to protect her family myth, to preserve the portrait she'd painted of herself for others to respect and admire. As years passed we fabricated a fortress of dishonesty, compounding emotional walls constructed during my childhood with adult lies until they became too tall to scale.

I was seven when Mother let me stay over night at my best friend, Sally's, for the first time. Sally, a first and only child whose father had died when she was two, was born when her mother, Ann, was forty-one, a rare reproductive miracle in 1948. Ann was a wind-in-the-hair-widow who rolled car windows all the way down, even in Michigan winter, and didn't care if we got dirty or ran through the house screaming. She let us burn our own hamburgers on her crumbling stone barbecue, glanced at the charred mess and hollered, "More catsup and mustard, they'll taste great." I still shut my eyes, smell that charcoal burnt meat and feel how it crunched against the roof of my mouth. I recall the invigoration of sprinting back and forth on worn oriental rugs in Ann's long living room, the comfort of collapsing and sprawling across cushy, faded furniture.

Yes, I've wondered how my life may have been different had I been born into Sally's household, just one door down from mine, if my obnoxious rebellion, fueled by the thrill of risk taking, may have been tempered.

Childhood lies were easy to get away with, like the one when

Sally and I were ten and lit up one of her mother's Chesterfield's. We'd been alone at her house, had choked and blown the smoke out the window but Mother smelled it when I came home. "You've been smoking and you're, well, you're becoming a juvenile delinquent." Juvenile delinquent? I'd heard the words on TV, on Dragnet, had deduced by the detective's voice that it must be bad, and was inspired by Mother's insult and gave her some lip. "I wasn't smoking, Sally's mother smokes. You know that." She backed off but for years sniffed me up and down whenever I came home from Sally's. I didn't smoke another cigarette until eleventh grade, but by then I had a steady boyfriend and had graduated to adult pleasures, ones with adult consequences requiring adult lies.

Mother confronted me the evening I'd ridden home with the top down in Tipp's dad's convertible. I was tousled and stinking of Stroh's when I tiptoed upstairs and she stormed out of her bedroom, face squeezing like a sponge. "You're a mess and you've been drinking. Have you let Tipp have his way with you?" Actually, I'd had it my way with Tipp, untied my ponytail, let my hair fly like a flag in the open convertible.

"Oh Mother, anyone looks like this after they ride with the top down and you'd know it if you weren't always worrying about your hairdo." Again, she backed off. Two friends, fellow members of the not-so-secret-society of bold girls at school, told me they'd recently admitted to having sex when confronted by their mothers. They said they didn't think they could stop doing it, and were taken to the doctor and birth control pills were prescribed. Their stories flabbergasted me. I couldn't fathom admitting my secret sex to Mother. Later, when I was five months pregnant and couldn't hide it, I didn't have to say a word.

How did I get comfortable with lying to Mother when I knew it was wrong? Dad, who set examples of consistent morality, taught me lying was wrong, and I'd gone to Methodist Sunday school since age six. In hindsight I see that his virtue, juxtaposed with Mother's harping, must have been daunting for a child. Dad didn't ask hard questions or put me in a position to lie, and instead complimented my accomplishments, repeating that I was capable of achieving anything. Even deceiving Mother, I thought. Perhaps I realized her model life was fabricated. To a boisterous child like me, it did seem unreal, the fairy-tale precision of her image.

A little girl who loves to run fast somehow knows it can't be done in high heels and my lying began in earnest with the revelation that I did not resemble my closest female role model and didn't want to. I released myself from that failure and protected myself with lies. I quit attempting to please a woman I'd never satisfied with stellar grades and impeccable piano recitals.

Years later, at about thirty-five, I evicted Mother from my mental castle and pulled up the drawbridge over the toxic emotion between us. We remained civil, and my lifetime close relationship with Dad, which may well have given me the strength to defy Mother, continued. Don't ask, don't tell. Yeah, well.

I was forty-one, long married and living across town, when Mother, then seventy-one, began inviting me out to Saturday lunch once a month. She insisted on driving and on picking up the tab each time we went out. I made a point of wearing makeup and something other than jeans, which she reminded me were appropriate only for farmers and hippies. We slid into a tacit understanding and certain subjects were taboo—my liberal politics, her staunch Methodism, music not suitable for performance by a community orchestra, why I wouldn't use the electric hair rollers she'd given me, and the so-called lurid lives of all film celebrities and rock stars. We'd stare across a two top at Machus Buffet, a restaurant that pleased Mother because she could see the food and comment on its quality before selecting her meal. We talked about the weather, if her friends colored their hair, what she'd found on sale at Hudson's, if the Salisbury steak was up to par.

I knew Mother was trying to establish an adult relationship with me, that polite small talk felt safe to her, and although I considered it, didn't risk opening up and telling her that my marriage was on its last legs. Instead, I nodded a lot, hoping to preserve the fragile détente between us. She kept calling and I kept going with her for over a year as rigid propriety and superficial conversation broke our hearts.

Mother's identity myth was blown to bits ten years ago, when my second husband, Don, and I took her to Florida to visit her last living sibling, younger brother, Joey. Halfway through dinner he referred to his Polish parents, how his kids, my cousins, had been fascinated by their Grandpa Jozef's stories about his harrowing escape from Russian Cossacks as Poland was further partitioned in 1906. Mother's fork of mashed potatoes flipped onto the floor. "Wait," I said, "Whose Polish parents?" Joey didn't miss a beat, tossed the verbal grenade. "Mine, and your mother's."

Mother hauled herself to her feet, tottered toward the Ladies Room and Joey filled in the blanks. He recounted Jozef's stealthy escape from his family's prosperous farm, how he'd fled by cover of night to Hamburg to avoid the Czar's spies in Gdansk, traveled in steerage and arrived at Ellis Island. He'd journeyed on to Crow Wing County, Minnesota where he labored in the taconite mines, saving money to send for my grandmother, Zofia and their fourteen-month-old son the following year.

Mother refused to discuss Joey's family revelations on the drive to the airport the next day. Instead, she described how *Today Show* host Katie Couric crossed her legs at the knees to show off trampy-looking shoes.

I called Joey a year after Mother died to verify that I'd understood him correctly during our dinner in Florida. He explained how disgusted Mother had been with their father, Jozef, who had lost his job at Ford when the plant cut workers in the 1930s. He was lucky to be cleaning streets and picking up garbage for the City of Detroit when Mother graduated with high honors. He had no money to resole his shoes, much less for college, even though two teachers had come to the house, advocating how intelligent and deserving she was. "Definitely the brightest of all nine of us kids," Joey said.

Joey recounted how Mother sobbed after her father refused her, how their bold mother, Zofia, who spoke little English, tromped off to the bus stop. Enlisting the help of a friendly bus driver, she'd ridden across town to the home of a wealthy woman whose laundry she'd been taking in for years. The Grosse Pointe woman gave Zofia money for one semester of college night school and all books for her brilliant daughter, even said she'd continue funding the education if Mother's grades were good, and they were. But Mother met Dad at her soda fountain job and her college dream was overridden by visions of security and marriage to a professional man.

During the same phone call with Joey, I asked why their parents weren't in Mother's wedding pictures. He hesitated. She had not invited them. He'd been the only family member allowed to attend because he'd agreed to change his name to Dale, just as Mother had, eight weeks before the wedding.

Back in third grade, when I'd questioned Mother about having other grandparents during our class family tree project, Zofia had been dead barely eight years, and my grandfather, Jozef, was alive and well. Retired from the Ford Rouge Plant, he was living thirty minutes away from us in Ferndale, where he remained until he died when I was eighteen.

I grieve now, five years after Mother's death, but not for her. She reinvented herself when she met Dad and stepped out of the scuffed boots of her childhood into the glossy high-heels of an upper middle class matron. She constructed the life she imagined and lived it. It's the lifetime of lies we told that makes me grieve, all the truth left unsaid between us, the mother-daughter opportunity that we missed. We lived twenty minutes apart for most of our lives, could have visited regularly, but didn't. She never told me her version of her life story and I still wonder if she was courageous or desperate.

Dad's deathbed request was that I take care of her for him, and I did, but it wasn't what she wanted. Or at least she acted as if it wasn't, calling out for everyone but me, the only person present at her bedside in the darkened hospital room. Still trying to understand what I couldn't undo, I slid first one, then the other, of her worn terrycloth slippers under her bed.

The Groves

Sandell Morse

Second Prize
Creative
Nonfiction

Dad was a photographer, but there are no pictures of those months in 1949 when we lived in Oak Hill, Florida, an orange grove town, a packing house town straddling U. S. 1. No photos of me sitting on an upside down orange crate in the back yard of Dad's hotel, petting Tiger, my striped orange cat. No photos of me riding my bike along a dirt road covered with oyster shells bleached white in the sun, passing palmetto trees and live oak dripping with clumps of Spanish moss thick like Brillo pads. I am ten. I will always be ten on that particular day, wearing a pair of white shorts, a white tee shirt, my curly dirty-blond hair wild and snarly. I'm pumping hard, following behind Cecil and Little Jimmy. Both boys wear jeans without belts. Their feet and chests are bare. Linette sits on the seat of Little Jimmy's bike. He pedals standing up. Her feet are bare, too. I'm the only kid in Oak Hill who wears shoes because my mother makes me. But I don't wear dresses. And I run wild, an animal child.

Memory brings back a narrow road barely wide enough for the pickup trucks that carry workers into the groves. Deep ditches flank both sides. Inside the grove, trees grow in rows as far as I can see. We pedal until we are deep inside those rows of trees, when suddenly Little Jimmy skids to a stop. Cecil does too. They ditch their bikes, race to claim trees. "This here's mine," Cecil yells.

"And this is mine," Little Jimmy yells back.

I'm prying at my kick stand with the toe of my brown oxford when Little Jimmy yells at me. "What're you doin' that for? Lay it down, stupid."

I'm not stupid, and I don't like people calling me stupid, especially not my dad, who says he's joking as if that made calling me names okay. *Hey, Stupes, what're you doing? Come over here, Stupes.* That word sets me off, and I want to get at Little Jimmy with my fists, but he's a mean kid, stronger and tougher than I am. The only reason I'm friends with him, if you can call it friends, is because Cecil's my boyfriend. Even then, as I kid, I think it's strange, having a boyfriend when I'm only in the fifth grade, especially a boyfriend like Cecil who's in the sixth grade. He stayed back twice, but I have to be his girlfriend, because, like I said, I'm not stupid and I understand that's the way things work here.

Linette is Little Jimmy's girlfriend. Sort of my friend. But not really. She's a quiet girl with thick brown hair that she wears in two braids. Once she stood on her kitchen table and danced for Little Jimmy, wearing just her underpants. I know because kids at school asked me if I was going to dance for Cecil. I shook my head, and I felt strange. I didn't know why.

In the grove, I drop my bike down into a ditch, figuring Cecil and Little Jimmy don't want chrome to glint. If somebody drives through, we'll see the truck from high up in our trees, then climb down, grab our bikes, ride fast and hide. Today, the groves are deserted and deeply quiet. I find a tree with a low crook, climb, reach for an orange, then pick releasing a shower of sound. Lowering myself to a branch, I bite into bitter rind, taste oil on my tongue. I suck juice, swing my legs, spit pits and here under the tree's canopy I can almost pretend I'm alone.

Writing now, I don't know how the fighting began, perhaps with voices, two boys shouting and taunting. Maybe Cecil and Little Jimmy started throwing oranges for no reason when one whizzed past my head, and I cried out. All these years later, and I'm still wondering. Memory erases Linette's image. Was she sitting on a low branch in Little Jimmy's tree. Did she have her own tree. Maybe, as I climbed higher trying to duck flying oranges, she climbed down her tree and left.

An orange hits my butt.

"Hey," I yell whirling about.

"Hey, yourself," Little Jimmy yells back.

He has brown hair, cut short and ragged. He hates it that way, but his father put a bowl on his head to guide the scissors. No kidding. I hurl an orange. It falls way short of Little Jimmy's tree and he laughs. A wiry kid, shorter than Cecil, he climbs like a monkey, fast and agile picking oranges as he goes, pausing then letting one fly. Balls of fruit thud against tree trunks, fall and splatter on the ground. Oranges hit leaves, hit me. Cecil throws, too, and now both boys are bombarding me. Why is Cecil throwing oranges at me? Why is he hitting me? What did I do to him? Yesterday, he gave me his marbles, tiger eyes, Aggies, clear crystals. He even asked me to marry him. No joke. That's what he said: "I want to marry you, Sandy."

"Stop it," I scream, "You're not funny, Cecil."

A rotten orange slams my tee shirt. I look down.

Little Jimmy yells, "Got your titties."

My hand flies to my chest, covering the orange stain. I don't have titties; I have tender swellings of my nipples. Do they know this? Through the leaves, I see them pointing and laughing. Another orange whizzes past my shoulder. Shielding my head, I duck oranges, then climb down, my right leg reaching for a lower branch when an orange smashes onto the V in front of my shorts.

Little Jimmy flings his arms over his head. "Bull's- eye."

I look like I peed my pants. "I hate you," I bellow. "I hate your rotten guts."

From his tree, Little Jimmy mocks me, his voice is high and squeaky like he's pretending he's a girl. "I hate you. Hate your rotten guts."

I need my bike. I can't find it. Where's my bike? Gone. A glint of chrome. I race toward it, but Cecil's behind me, and I hear his footsteps coming closer, feel his fingers grab my shirt. I turn, but he won't let go. Now his face is close to mine, and I smell his sweet rotten-orange breath, his muskiness. He has black hair with a strand that falls over his forehead. He tosses it back with a snap of his neck. I spray saliva into his face, my words hard. "Let me go."

Hooking a foot around my ankle, he wrestles me to the ground then straddles my waist. "Take it back."

Fury and fear twist like a rope in my belly. I really do hate his lousy guts. "Take what back? What did I say?"

"You know."

"Don't either."

"Liar."

"I'm not a liar and you know it."

His black hair is soaked with sweat, matting along his temples. His eyes glare. I've never seen him look so mean. He snorts. "Bitch."

I shiver. "I'll take it back."

He grabs a rotten orange, lifts it high, then grins. "Too late."

I thrust my body up under his. He tightens his thighs. There is something warm inside his jeans. And soft. Then bone. What is that warmth? Why is he pushing so low on my body? I have one free hand. Making a claw out of my fingers, I'm ready to rake my nails down his cheek when the orange comes down, pulp filling my mouth and my nostrils. I struggle to breathe. I feel squishy. Like a snail without a shell.

Standing off to one side, Little Jimmy jiggles marbles in his front pocket and he shrieks, "Give it to her. Give it good."

Linette is gone.

My arm flails and my eyes are so wide I feel them stretching. I need air. Really need air. Sensing that something is going terribly wrong, Cecil heaves the orange into the trees, but he doesn't let go. I'm pinned. Tears spill. "I'm telling my father. He'll fix you."

Cecil bounces, and I squirm under that warmth inside his trousers. His eyes narrow. "That right?"

But I've already seen a flicker of fear.

He loosens his hold, and I wiggle out, running fast for my bike.

"Get her, get her," Little Jimmy wails. "Come on. Let's go."

"Aw, let her be," Cecil mumbles.

I pedal hard. My front wheel swerves, skims the wall of a ditch and I pull back just in time. Narrow wooden bridges span these drainage ditches. Cecil, Little Jimmy and Linette live back there. You can't see those places from the road, but that's where most of the kids in my school live in unpainted wooden shacks with water pumps in their dooryards out-houses in back. I'm one of eight kids in the fifth grade, sharing a room with the sixth, the teacher walking back and forth. I'm a middle class Jewish kid who mostly grew up in New Jersey before Dad moved us to Florida, first Hollywood, then Oak Hill. I don't belong here. Mom knows that; I know that. Not Dad. He's making money renting rooms to men who come to fish the Indian River, to tourists driving to Miami Beach, then stopping purposely on their way back because Dad's such a card, and he serves a the best fried chicken in his restaurant, a café with a picture window looking out on the highway, a sign painted on the glass: Café: Home Cooking. Friday nights when the juke box blares, the restaurant turns into a tavern, Dad selling beer in long necked brown bottles and chances on his punch cards. Punch cards are a gambling game, and as Dad knows, the odds go to the house.

In the café, Dad's a regular Master of Ceremonies moving, seamlessly, from table to table telling jokes, sitting and schmoozing. Folks like him. He's Yul Brenner handsome, high cheekbones, strong jaw, tall with square shoulders. Sometimes, before bed, when I sit on his lap in the restaurant on those Friday nights, the men watch me, then lift their beer bottles and say how pretty I am. Dad smiles. I smile, too, because I'm making him proud. Mom says the café is no place for me with all that noise and beer drinking. "What's wrong with it?" Dad says.

She looks away.

Holding the handle bars, I wheel my bike and dash across the highway which breaks Dad's rule. I broke lots of his rules that day; playing in the groves, crossing the highway without calling for Mom to guide me. Standing inside the still and strangely quiet air in front of the hotel—no insects, no eighteen wheelers rumbling past—I feel suspended. Should I turn right or left? Dash past the lobby or past the café's picture window? Dad could be anywhere. I need to get to the center door in the back, then to my room. At first, I don't see him, but he's there, standing and smoothing his bald head with his palm. "Going someplace?"

I'm watching that hand, ready to duck if it shoots out, hardly listening to his shouts. "Where have you been? Look at you, you're an animal."

I look at my oxfords, my balled up socks slipping down into the heels of my shoes, my dirty ankle bones, a scratch bleeding.

"You're a mess," he says, his voice all sour and mean. "What the hell happened to you?"

I want to fall into his arms, to tell him that Little Jimmy and Cecil were attacking me, that Cecil sat on my belly and something I couldn't understand was happening, but I didn't have words. How can I explain what I don't know? And looking back, I realize Dad wouldn't have listened. He wouldn't have understood. What is about to happen is inevitable. I squeeze out a single word. "They…"

He interrupts. "Always the other guy. Never you."

"I'm trying to explain."

"So explain."

I shake my head.

"I'm waiting."

My tongue fills my mouth.

He grabs the front of my tee shirt and pulls me close, holding his face close to mine. The toes of my shoes barely touch the ground, but I'm still holding onto my bike, still squeezing the hand grips. "Did you cross the highway? Did you?"

I stammer. "I… I had to."

"Without calling for your mother? How many times do I have to tell you the same thing? You want to get yourself killed? You think those truck drivers will see you? Answer me. Why don't you answer me?"

I can't speak.

He lets go pushing hard. I lose my balance, and I fall. My bike crashes, the wheel spinning. I'm crying now. He doesn't care.

"Now, go to your room and stay there."

Resting my chin on the window sill, I stare into the backyard, a patchwork of red dirt and wide-bladed Florida grass growing in clumps, all of it bordered with thick jungle where palmetto trees and live oak grow, their branches dripping with clumps of Spanish moss thick like Brillo pads. Panthers and coral snakes live back there. A path cuts through to my school, but I don't want to go to that school ever again. I don't want to see Little Jimmy or Cecil. I hate their guts. I want Tiger, our cat. She's outside, sitting tall on her upside down orange crate, lifting a paw and licking the underside with her long pink tongue. She wears a collar with a rope that Dad attaches to the crate. He's the only person I know who ties a cat. Nights, he puts her in the restaurant where she catches mice. He says that's all she's good for. But Tiger is my friend, and sometimes when I'm sad or lonely, I burrow my face into her fur until she purrs. It's what I want to do now. Desperately. But Tiger's not allowed in my room.

I don't know how long I've been waiting, but I can see the light casting a shadow beside the orange crate. I'm getting hungry. Has he forgotten me? Is he busy? He's always busy. *Don't bother me, Sandy. Can't you see I'm busy?* Tiger jumps down from her crate and stretches long. She humps her back. Then, I hear his footsteps in the corridor. He's moving slowly and torturing me. If I could, I'd turn myself into a ghost and slip through the tiny holes in the screen, untie Tiger and disappear. The shiny round doorknob turns, and he's inside, closing the door behind him, leaning back, his beady eyes glaring. "How many times do I have to tell you, Sandy? You think I don't know where you were? You think I like it when I go into Alderman's Store and old man Alderman tells me he saw you riding into the groves like some hooligan. You think you can just pick those oranges? You think they're yours? They're a man's livelihood."

He grabs an arm, pulls me to my feet. "You're no better than a common thief."

I'm trying to pull away, but he has a good hold. I figure maybe if I say I'm sorry, I'll be okay, so I tell him I didn't mean it. "I didn't know."

He mocks me. "You didn't know. So now you're a liar, too?"

"Daddy, I'm sorry. I'm really sorry."

He spits words. "You're no good, you hear me? A piece of trash."

I look down at the orange starburst at the V of my shorts, that private place Mommy tells me I must not touch, that no one must touch. Does he see the stain where Little Jimmy hit me with a rotten orange, then lifted his arms above his head, shouting Bull's-eye? Shame and anger swirl in my belly, in my brain, and I'm so mixed up, I start to cry.

He narrows his eyes. "Don't pull that crap on me."

I stare at his fingers and I can't believe what I'm seeing. He's unbuckling his belt, taking his time, pulling the long tongue through loops. I hear the sound of his breathing, of my breathing. I gulp air. What if I wet my pants? "I want Mommy."

He curls his upper lip. "You want Mommy."

The belt comes down, and I scream. "Stop it."

"Stop what?"

Some terrible rhythm takes hold of him as he brings the belt down, over and over. I'm scrambling along the linoleum floor, pressing my knobby backbone into a corner, sitting with my knees drawn up and my arms folded over my head, sobbing so hard my teeth ache. He pulls me to my feet, his breath coming in short, hard puffs. "Teach... lesson... once... for all."

A rush and roar inside my head. "I want Mommy. "

Where is she? Where is my mother? Did he yell at her? Threaten her? Send her across the street to Alderman's to buy meat for the restaurant? Does she know his belt is whirling like a hurricane?

I hold my breath, and it takes me an instant to realize he's not hitting. The air goes still. Nothing moves. Peering out from under my arms, I see his chest heave, hear his breath, loud and ragged. His face looks strange as if his thoughts have taken him far away. Is he going to hit me again? Turn and leave? Fingers trembling, he threads the belt through loops, then buckles. "You think you're my daughter?" he says to me. "Well, think again."

I want him. I want my father. All of my life I will want my charming, abusive, angry, charismatic, volatile father. "Don't say that," I scream.

He laughs.

That laugh does it. Now I'm mad, really mad. Standing, I stomp my foot. "I'm leaving."

"Is that so?"

"Yes, that's so."

He laughs, again. "You think I care?"

He shouldn't be talking to me like that. I'm his kid. More his kid at that moment than I realize because I'm setting my fake alligator overnight bag on my bed, opening the brass catches. Inside, the paper that lines the lid is the color of a summer sky, and seeing that blue, I nearly burst into tears because deep inside, I know I'm a child with no place to go. But I'm not ready to say that. A light weight jacket hangs in my closet. I reach, and just then Dad's hand pulls the jacket from a hanger. "Here," he says, "I'll help you pack."

Cars and trucks speed past spraying sound, spraying grit. The highway is flat with two lanes, a sandy shoulder where I walk heading for the

Greyhound stop. You have to flag the driver. I know how because I've watched Mom. She doesn't drive, and when we need to shop, we ride the bus to New Smyrna Beach where Mom buys me new dungarees, buys herself a white blouse, looking in a three-way mirror in a dressing room and asking how I like it. Does she look good? On those days, we sit at the lunch counter in Woolworths, Mom drinking a cup of coffee—how Mom loved her coffee—me sipping cherry Coke. She doesn't get mad and tell me to hurry up when I sip slowly through my straw, making sweetness last. I love Mom, but I can't have her when Dad's around because she belongs to him, and so on that day when I am ten, I know exactly where I'm going, back to New Jersey where I belong. Mom has three brothers; one will take me in.

Next to this empty place where the bus pulls in, tall grasses and cat tails grow in murky water. Lots of murky water in Oak Hill, ditches and swamps where I play, cutting down cat tails and lighting the ends with matches. I know I'm not supposed to, but that's what kids do here. Eight of us in the fifth grade, sharing a room with the sixth, the teacher walking back and forth in front. I'm so bored I do the lessons for both grades.

Kicking dirt with the toe of my oxford, I look north toward the hotel just in case Mom is coming. Where is she? Maybe, she doesn't know. Wouldn't that be terrible, me boarding the bus and Mom finding out later I was gone? I'm still wearing my stained white shorts, stained tee shirt. What will the bus driver say? I'll tell him I have to meet Mom in New Symerna Beach. Suddenly, my welts itch like crazy, but scratching burns. Flat and empty inside, I pick up the scent of oranges, of Cecil's muskiness, and I feel that softness between his legs, see the bulge in his trousers. I almost know what those things are, but not quite. Is Cecil here? I'm too afraid to look.

Mom says bad things happen to girls. Dad says girls need to watch out. *Don't take candy from strangers. If someone asks you for directions, stay on the curb.* Like we have curbs in Oak Hill. *Don't walk to the car. Better, yet, say you don't know and run home.* Dad doesn't exactly say, but I understand if something bad happens to me it will be, as he says, my own damn fault.

Shading my eyes, I search for the Greyhound's tall shadowy shape. I'm worried. Could I have missed it? *Please, bus, please come.*

Lowering my gaze, I count to sixty before looking again. Another sixty. Nothing but cars in the distance and a big eighteen wheeler rushing, then whooshing past. Blue bleeds from the sky, and vultures circle, the tips of their wings pointing like fingers. What do they see? I used to think vultures were hawks; then Cecil showed me a row of them sitting on a roof beam. Such ugly birds with their humping wings, red heads, thick beaks and beady eyes, just sitting and doing nothing, not even feeding on something dead.

A breeze stirs the air as clouds mass. Rain comes fast in Florida. I want the bus; I need the bus. *If I see three blue cars in a row, the bus will come. If I look north instead of south, the bus will come.* The sky turns dark. There's a house nearby where a woman sells cloth she cuts from bolts, but there's a closed sign in her window. Besides, there's no porch, no where to stand out of the rain. I stumble, and my suitcase falls.

Then, I see her hurrying along the sandy shoulder, her short, square body heading into the wind, tilting like the prow of a ship. She has wiry salt and pepper hair, and that hair is blowing. Lifting an arm, she calls my name: "Sandy." A gust of wind sprays sand, and I turn away, shielding my eyes. She calls again. "Wait, Sandy. Wait."

And I do that, wait. Where will I go? Nowhere. Who was I kidding, keeping my eyes peeled for a bus that did not come, would not come? She's still hurrying, getting closer, so close, I see the furrows in her brow. Her lip twists. Something in her face has collapsed. Even her skin looks deflated, and her eyes—so sad. They've been fighting. Mom has trouble with Dad, too, the way he yells, screams and rants. I'm not the only one he calls, Stupid. He makes Mom feel worthless, too, and although I will remember every detail of that day, the smell of oranges, the way I longed for Tiger, Dad's belt coming down on my wing bones, Dad's true legacy will be his slow erosion of my essence, my very soul, and for that, I will never forgive him. Lowering my chin, I lift my suitcase. Mom reaches for the handle, and I let her take it. Neither of us speaks as we walk side by side, rain falling in quarter size drops. One day I'll leave, really leave, and I won't go back. Ever.

What to Expect While Grieving for Your Father

Hannah Karena Jones

Honorable
Mention
Creative
Nonfiction

Usually, the first question people ask is how long it's going to take before they "get over it." How long until the thought of his absence stops crippling your knees in elevators, before the realization of his permanent departure stops punching you in the stomach each morning as you slip into closed-eyes consciousness. I have this theory that if you know it's coming—if your Dad's been dying for a week, a month, a year—if you've had time to prepare for it then you can slash that much off the total recovery time.[1] Out of the blue fatal car crashes take longer to "get over" because they're sudden.

I had three days.

Expect to cry at the snap of anyone's fingers—friends, family, strangers, bus drivers—for two weeks or so.

The first few nights he's gone, well after everyone else has cried themselves to sleep, don't be surprised when you turn the TV on full volume before scurrying barefoot back to your pillows. Late night news programs have been your bedtime story and your lullaby for years. When your mother tells you to knock it off because it's both annoying and a waste of electricity, decide to either wean yourself off the habit, or set your alarm for 4 A.M. and turn the TV off before she wakes up.

Expect to realize, in the handful of days before the funeral, that you're an orphan, or at least half an orphan. Feel shocked. Study orphan movies like *Annie* and *Oliver Twist* and figure out how to alter your behavior to put on the proper performance for the rest of your fatherless life. During the third or fourth dance number, you'll wonder if you need to learn how to sing for your supper. You never could sing. Dad says it isn't in our genes.

Said. He *said* it wasn't in our genes. Grow accustomed to correcting yourself and replacing present progressive verbs with the past tense.

Also, expect to hate all television characters who have living fathers and don't appreciate them with a parade and chipped beef on rye toast for breakfast, like he asks, even if the salted-cream smell of it makes you gag. It would have been such a small sacrifice. Not enough to pick a fight over.

Avoid watching any films with weddings in them. Cry over how, at your own wedding, your father won't be walking you down the aisle.

You'll wonder how your future fiancé will propose. Will he ask your Mom for permission instead? Or will he skip the whole tradition entirely? You never have to admit to yourself that you found the whole practice antiquated and sexist before your father died. That you had hoped you'd find a man who popped the question because he loved you and damn your father's opinion. You're entitled to feel a sense of loss over something you never even wanted in the first place because now you can't have it anyway. And that's not fair.

After a few months you'll emotionally graduate to watching wedding dress reality shows. You like them. The dresses are beautiful and you'll even allow yourself to imagine your own lace gown without simultaneously worrying over how odd it will look as you walk yourself down the aisle and give yourself away.

Do not, at all costs, go to church on Father's Day Sunday. The sermon will without fail always be about gratitude for your Dad. Either you can sit, your Sunday makeup leaking so loud everyone in the hushed pews notices, or you can try to excuse yourself, knocking into sheer stocking knees and dripping snot onto their family Bibles. They'll notice anyway.

* * *

Expect, after a year and half or so, to catch yourself subconsciously searching for a significant male figure. He will not replace your father, but rather maintain some of the practices. You won't realize until this new man does it that you've missed being praised for good grades, being bragged about to grocery store managers. He can be a relative, a teacher, your boyfriend's dad. Bonus points, though, if he's related to your own deceased father because he looks like him and, on occasion, will tell you stories you've never heard about their childhoods together and he can retell the stories that you're beginning to forget, the details and facts growing fuzzy around the edges.

Accept—and give permission—that your mother may date, but constantly compare each man to your father. When she falls in love again, you'll remind her that she can, and has, done better. "Don't settle," you'll tell her as she smears on crusty lipstick last used on what was supposed to be her last date.

Have fights with younger siblings who don't remember the story behind the antique fishing reel exactly the same way you do. Storm out of the room when they insist his favorite flavor of ice cream was Strawberry instead of Cherry Garcia. Start a themed lecture series to refresh their memories on the correct facts and tell them how your grandfather almost bought a ticket to Australia instead of America when he immigrated in 1910. It's a story which they mistakenly insist Dad never told them. Have them recite it back, word for word, until it's seared into their brains. "It's family history," you explain patiently when they whine for a break. "It's important you remember it right."

You'll emphasize the preservation of all these mundane details because you know that you're not getting over his death. You are not starting to feel better. You're just starting to forget.

---

[1] Concerning other issues, such as estrangement or outright mutual hatred, feel free to knock the amount of years you've wished him dead and gone off the E.R.T. (Estimated Recovery Time).

NOVELLA

Judged by Robin Miura

First Prize: Stephanie Coyne DeGhett of Potsdam, NY
for *Hazzard's*

Honorable Mention: Nicole Louise Reid of Newburgh, IN
for *A Purposeful Violence*

2012
PRESS 53
OPEN AWARDS

Finalists:

Laurie Blauner of Seattle, WA for *Earl*

M.A. Tuohy of Buford, GA for *Double Nickel Jackpot*

Steve Yates of Flowood, MS for *Sandy and Wayne*

Hazzard's

Stephanie Coyne DeGhett

First Prize
Novella

The four-stroke gasoline engine derives its energy from heat generated by combustion within its cylinder. The strokes required to complete the operation are intake, compression, power and exhaust. Hazzard's New Engine Repair Guide, 1957. Page 25.

STROKE 1: INTAKE

She stood in the kitchen in the late-day light, resisting a surge of panic. Her bead shop sold, her apartment given up. Her old hatchback wagon filled with her belongings, a torch, a 24-drawer carpenter's cabinet full of beads and fastenings and an annealing kiln that looked like a red enamel toolbox or a toaster oven. Frankie was just beginning to take it all in—the remoteness, the ocean, the need to figure out how to feed herself. Time to call Simon St. John, she thought, and admit renting his cousin's old place wouldn't work out after all.

Frankie heard the air horn of the departing ferry sound in the distance as it cleared the cove beyond the first buoy. If she wanted to leave now, she'd have to swim for it, all eight miles. She had gotten rid of everything, including a way out. She had driven across three states to the dry edge of the continent. Then over the edge. And wasn't this what she had wanted? Not this expanse of blue ocean—she'd never even seen the Atlantic before—or even this small island off the coast of Maine, but the sense of disconnect from the mainland or any notion of mainland. To spend some time separate, like an unstrung bead. To try her luck a new way, transforming a chicken coop into an island studio.

Her footfalls echoed in the chilly, empty kitchen of her new place, her artist's retreat. She was hungry. The big white fridge, of course, was empty. She remembered those minivans full of brown paper bags of groceries pulling onto the ferry. She wished she had stocked up on frozen pizza, except now she could see there wasn't even a freezer in this house. Back in Vermont, the answer had been the take-out place down the alley from the shop she had owned in Burlington.

Stay focused on getting ready for the New England Bead Show in Boston, she thought. Around her neck she was wearing a linen cord and on it was a large, intricate bead, one she had created in the flame of her torch. The bead that, flaws and all, had been the beginning of believing she could be a bead artist. Encased in layers of transparent glass were bits of silver leaf and wisps of green and blue that had gone molten. She tugged it right and left in a short arc under her chin as she looked around, getting the measure of her new circumstances.

From the window in the kitchen door, she looked out on the rocky, sloping side yard. There was the former chicken coop that Simon had mentioned and that until now had been the promising notion of "studio" in her mind: now it was a low shed with a slight cant and a sagging door. She turned away from the view to survey the kitchen. Here, beside the gas stove was a bureau, a random interlock of scorch rings across its varnished top. She jerked open a drawer: frying pans, paper bags, a plastering knife with an offset handle, a nail apron, empty coffee cans, several old spark plugs, and a propane canister nozzle clanked against each other.

She had rented this place sight unseen and Simon St. John had called it "sparse but complete." Complete? She inspected the old chinaware in the cupboard. It was fine—but the rest of the kitchen was equipped with remnants of a workshop and a recycle bin. Not even a can opener. This defied any notion of make-do. And there was no kitchen re-outfitting to do: she had a year's rental and not quite a year's money. The woman whose kitchen this had been had apparently managed in her own way. So would she.

Upstairs, Frankie chose a bedroom. From it, in the distance, she could see the harbor and its wharf and clusters of white and yellow houses on the spruce hillside above the shore. The room was sparsely furnished—a bed, a nightstand, a trunk and a sprawl of books on the floor. She moved them aside with her foot, dumping her beader's sketchbook and a big handful of colored pencils wrapped in a rubber band into the trunk. Reaching down, she flipped some of the books over: cookbooks. Of course, she thought, bureau in the kitchen, cookbooks in the bedroom. Frankie couldn't cook and there wasn't a single ingredient on her pantry shelf.

Among the cookbooks was a fifty-year-old car repair manual. Maybe that she could use. Her twenty-year old car paused—like some kind of synaptic gasp—sometimes when she stepped hard on the gas pedal. She had learned not to try to pass in any kind of tight circumstance, but the lurch was finding new times to manifest itself. She would have to take it in to get it looked at when she had some cash. Take the car in? she thought. Where on Ile du Nord could she do that? Was there even a gas station on the island? There were practical details to living in this place that she hadn't considered. Then, trying to draw breath against the near-vacuum in her chest, she concentrated on her most immediate problem: her first meal on this island.

Ile du Nord was six miles long between its most distant points and its granite-rimmed coastline was deeply irregular. Basic geography was all, really, that she knew. There was a library and one store; these she had passed. Simon had said there would be an island restaurant with take-out near the wharf and lobster pound, but not until summer. It was only late April. Suddenly alive to the idea that the little store might close, Frankie headed for the car and wheeled out onto the road. The little wagon lurched into a hiccough as Frankie accelerated out of the driveway, making the back tires spit a little spray of gravel when it took off. The gas gauge said over half a tank, enough to do this twisting ribbon of island roads for a while, she thought with relief, narrowly missing a rusty white jeep banking wide around the bend from the other direction. Its driver waved.

The placard on Corinne's Island Store still said OPEN when Frankie pushed through the door. She looked around, grateful, and began to take the place in. There was a long aisle of hardware before the reassuring processions of canned food and boxed mixes began. Just inside the door was a big bulletin board: a bottle drive, someone interested in sharing ferry expenses to have a septic system pumped out, roosters for sale. The library had posted a sign-up sheet for volunteers for its renovation project. She could put up her own notice: *Classes For Macramé Bracelets and Beaded Book Thongs.* She was going to need the money.

Walking down an aisle, she flipped a can over: the price was huge. Of course. Either pay to take the ferry over yourself or pay to have the ferry deliver it. Caught in coordinates of her cooking abilities and her finances, she bought a box of cereal at a fabulous price—and soup. Won't soup work, she wondered, finding herself hungrier by the moment. A bag of apples. She could do this after all. In a stroke of sheer open vision, she grabbed a can opener and made her way to the register.

On the wall by the checkout counter there was an old framed black-and-white photograph of the ferry at the Ile du Nord dock and a line up of men in front of it: *First run of the Ile du Nord Ferry, 1955* was typed on a strip of paper glued across the bottom. Imagine this place with no ferry, she thought with a stab of appreciation for the new isolation she had sought and found.

"You come from away," said the woman who approached the register. "Where are you staying?"

Corinne, thought Frankie, this must be Corinne. The storekeeper was a decade older than she was, she guessed, late thirties, maybe early forties. Interesting earrings—hammered silver hoops—hanging from each ear. And tall, tall enough that the store, with its somewhat low ceilings and short aisles, looked slightly too small for her.

"St. John's house," Frankie answered. "Off Quarry Road."

"So you're the artist who's got Old Chris's place—how long did you take it for?"

"A year," she answered, wondering how many cans she'd have ground open on her new can opener by then and how this woman knew who she was.

"Amazing bead," said the woman, glancing at Frankie's necklace as she bagged the groceries.

"Lampworked," said Frankie, touching her flawed talisman. "Made with a torch."

"So you're a bead artist?"

Frankie nodded and said, "Here to work on a project." She pulled the elastic from her auburn hair and remade her short ponytail, still spilling wisps, and reached for the bag.

"Welcome to the island, bead artist," said Corinne, and introduced herself. "Old Chris's house has been empty too long.

Here," she added, sliding a small box of spiral pasta toward Frankie. "Sprinkle some of this in that tomato soup when you cook it and it won't look so sorrowful."

"Thanks," said Frankie, rattling the small shapes inside the box. Then she said, "Somebody in a white Jeep waved at me."

"That old Jeep—it's a miracle Lennie still runs it. Lennie's your landlord's cousin, Old Chris's, too. I bet he's a little surprised Simon finally rented the place out. I think Lennie might have wanted his sister's boy to have it for the summer."

"Why did he wave at me?"

"Everyone waves here."

As Frankie headed out the door, Corinne called out, "Be careful when you light the oven in Old Chris's stove—the pilot light is tricky."

The whole domestic side of this little adventure is tricky, thought Frankie. Did Corinne know about everyone's appliances or had she and Old Chris spent time in each other's kitchens? Frankie had never spent much time in kitchens, but apparently she was going to have to get used to this one.

Once home, she pulled her canvas tool bag out of the car and dumped her beading tools in the bureau drawer. *Bead artist*, she thought. Not beader. Not a genetics lab tech with a hobby that had overtaken her kitchen. Not a bead shop owner assembling kits for summer workshops in earring making for teenagers. Rummaging for a saucepan, Frankie held up a wrench from the drawer in one hand, then balanced a pair of her own needle-nose pliers in the other. Had Old Chris been a big woman or small, like her? Probably bigger, she thought, hefting the wrench. She closed the drawer, put her new can opener on top of the scorched bureau. Miles out to sea on a knob of spruce and rock, Frankie laid claim to the kitchen.

She lit the blue-and-yellow flame of the front burner and put the water on for the pasta. While it heated, Frankie began to unpack her clothes: the bundle that was her heavy brown overalls for working with hot glass had met a sticky fate en route. Stashed under the driver's seat, they had soaked up a spill of soda. The ancient washer in Old Chris's stone cellar still worked, but there was no dryer and Frankie peered along the shelves under the single bulb illumination until she spotted a spool of thick, fluorescent pink-red, nylon-coated, 14-gauge electrical wire. It was just barely supple enough to knot and twist between a big hook screwed into the corner of the house and the apple tree. No clothespins, of course, thought Frankie, marveling at the unexpected demands of island life in its first moments. She would have to fasten the straps of her overalls over the line. "How did you make it work here, Old Chris?" she asked aloud.

Frankie found herself curled up in the bedroom with a mug of tomato soup afloat with fusilli, checking out the spines of a stash of abandoned cookbooks. What a mocking trick these are, she thought. She would drop them off at Simon's. If he didn't want them, she'd have a yard sale, if they did that kind of thing on Ile du Nord. Twenty-seven cookbooks, $13.50. Didn't even amount to ferry money. And even if she could afford a mainland ferry run, could she trust herself not to keep heading west? She would send a postcard: *Sorry, Simon, couldn't make a go of Old Chris's kitchen.*

Gabe would love this little irony, she thought, looking at her cookbook inheritance. But she wasn't going to tell her brother anything, not yet. If he mocked her bead business, imagine what he was going to say about bead making in an island studio. Frankie usually told Gabe too much. And what she didn't tell him, he often intuited with deadly accuracy. During the winter he'd known without her saying that she was living alone again. Maybe she hadn't used the word "we" in awhile.

"What's the story with the boyfriend," Gabe had begun when he called from back in Ohio months ago while she was at Mother of Pearl's, her little side street shop. "You get rid of him or he get rid of you?"

Frankie had bristled. "I showed him the way out, Gabe, and he took it."

"What did you do? Cook for him and let events solve themselves?"

"You can't fix a meal, either," she countered.

"Okay, so no boyfriend. So what now?" Gabe taunting in his usual way. Three years older, Gabe had taken on his big brother status as a piece of identity—protective, filling in all the gaps left by parents who were distracted by their work. When she and Gabe were kids, that had meant providing her with lunches in the summer and letting her choose chicken noodle soup as often as she wanted. His bag of tricks for herding her away from harm and toward whatever he thought was good for her hadn't grown much more sophisticated since he was nine and bringing all his playground techniques to bear on the task he had set himself with his little sister. He bribed sometimes, but mostly provoked and bullied her into safety. Gabe was the one who had driven her to college her first year. A dozen hours and more in the car. When they arrived in Burlington, he unpacked her gear, grabbed a campus map and found the cafeterias and the library with her and then stood with her in line to get her orientation packet. "Don't screw it up," he said and got back in the car and drove himself all the way back to Ohio where classes for his senior year started the next day.

And, on the phone, he had been mustering his usual techniques. "Your life's in great shape," he said. "First you give up the research lab because it isn't quite right. All that schooling! All for a bead shop! Now the boyfriend isn't quite right, after all. Maybe you should keep trading what almost works for nothing at all? Maybe swap your nearly successful business selling trinkets and beach glass for unemployment? Get rid of your apartment and become a neo-hermit?"

The idea had appeal.

"But, no," her brother was saying, "you'll keep that apartment because it's so close to Luck Street you can see it from your window. And that's where you want to be, just in sight of luck, but not quite there."

Gabe's devastating sense of geography was right: her apartment was less than a block away from Luck Street. Suddenly, she had wanted to be very far away.

And now she was.

She spread the cookbooks and the one maverick engine repair guide out. The first one she picked up was *365 Soups and How to Prepare Them*. A string of answers to every evening on Ile du Nord. Inside, on a page margin, a buttery old finger print. "Hey, Old Chris," she said, touching it with her own finger. Written inside the front cover was a recipe for Southwinds: yeast-raised rolls made like doughnuts, in hot oil, to be eaten on the spot, with butter. And next to it, a note: *Serve with Poor Man's Soup.* She flipped to the index, but Poor Man's was not there.

Frankie picked up the car repair manual: *Hazzard's New Engine Repair Guide.* The smell of gasoline or oil or both clung to it faintly, a little sharp in her nose, but not unpleasant. A gas station smell, the smell of going somewhere. She remembered filling up early that morning at the convenience store's pumps, all six of them busy under their low canopy. The penetrating smell of fuel, the grumbling of an idling truck. That all seemed unimaginably remote.

Hazzard's was thick with a supple leatherette cover and shopworn pages that had an odd fanning to them. Taped into it were specs for a shed and a diagram for a set of porch stairs. There were instructions for the water heater. Scribbled in the margins and on the back pages were phone numbers and parts numbers. One page listed the fuse numbers and layout for the electrical junction box in the cellar. Frankie had the impression that Old Chris had covered all the bases for getting by on Quarry Road in her marginal notes.

She thumbed the pages and saw several folded newspaper articles, some hand-written notes and two ancient four-leaf clovers. And there were recipes, some cut from magazines, some written on scrap paper and tucked in or glued in. The first recipe in *Hazzard's* was one for crêpes, which she thought sounded pretty fancy for a car repair manual, and the next one she found was a transcription of the recipe for Southwinds. It was on page 25: "How a Gas Engine Works." Taped beneath that, a piece of neatly torn yellowed paper listed the ingredients: yeast, flour, an egg, a little salt, a little sugar, warm milk. Underneath the name of the recipe Old Chris had written *Maggie's Recipe.* Beside it, a note that read *only the pan with the dent is big enough for this.*

Pasted over the text on page 26 came the soup recipe she had wanted to find, except this recipe was called Poor Woman's Soup instead of Poor Man's. Better yet, she thought. Carrots, onions, barley, a little ground beef. Oregano. Maybe pasta, Frankie thought, something pretty. Maybe shells. Maybe something gorgeous and green, like celery or a handful of beans. Maybe she could even fix this meal—Southwinds and the soup she had just discovered. Its modest ambition fit her willingness and sudden need for a meal with ingredients. *Cook till done,* the soup recipe concluded, *You'll know when that is.* Maybe she would trust Old Chris and try this out.

Frankie put aside her mug of soup, unfinished. The image of hot rolls bobbing up golden in their oil and steaming as they broke open to a snowy white filled her hungry mind.

Stroke 2. Compression

Frankie was making her way in another woman's kitchen. One of the only things she had added besides the new can opener was an array of pasta, all the kinds Corinne carried, poured into big glass jars. Charms against hunger. She was glad of the traces of Old Chris, including the nail apron she had found in the drawer when she was cooking—confirmation someone else had gotten through meals here.

All her apartments had had tiny kitchens that had immediately become workshops. When she opened the bead shop, she had stored inventory in her kitchen cabinets, stashing boxes and vials and packets full of her tiny inventory into her cupboards until there was no room for anything but a box or two of cereal, a few boxes of herbal tea and a stack of ramen noodles. She could have concocted a bead casserole or a clasps-and-findings stew, but dinner always came out of the glass-doored freezer at the North End Market.

Old Chris St. John's kitchen was big and there was no reason to turn it into her make-do studio. Now she remembered how empty a kitchen could feel. The one she and her brother had grown up in had looked as if it had been assembled from cooking catalogues and arranged by movers who had put appliances on the counters in a near-random way on moving day. Only by the microwave and the toaster did drawer handles show wear and cupboard panels have the smudges of ordinary use. There, in a cluster, were things in easy reach: the spreading knife for margarine, the cereal in the cabinets below, the bowls on the shelves above. The room had retained the quality of seeming to wait for its owners to arrive for her whole growing up, right up until a year ago when she returned to Ohio to help Gabe clean out their parents' house.

"It's a wonder the place didn't explode." That's what someone from Dayton's fire department team had said. He had been among those who had answered the call when her parents died: the furnace had malfunctioned; slowly, as her parents slept, gas had replaced nearly every molecule of oxygen.

There never was enough air here, she had thought, looking around the kitchen. She knew from experience no one could breathe simple emptiness. Plastic garbage bags filled with contents from the cupboards leaned against the cupboards.

"What's sadder," asked Frankie, "twenty-two boxes of mac and cheese or seventeen boxes of unused appliances?" Cuisinart food mill, trigger-start aluminum chef's torch, electric knife.

Gabe claimed the knife and turned to put it in the small pile of things he was taking back to his apartment with him. In his old rugby shirt and khakis, he didn't look so different from the kid she had shared so many childhood lunches with in this kitchen.

"The one time Dad used that he turned the ham to pudding," said Frankie.

"Never mind. Here, at least take the Cuisinart," said her brother, kicking at the wall of boxes, some with their staples still intact. "It was Mom's, after all."

She pictured the big food processor commandeering space in her tiny converted workshop-kitchen in Vermont. Preposterous, she thought, but agreed. As Gabe carried a box into the dining room, she reached across the counter and grabbed the faintly gummy old electric can opener, thunking it into the trash. Goodbye, Mom, she thought.

Waiting for Gabe, Frankie had slid her back down the cabinet and sat on the linoleum. Then, she reached behind her into the closest door, took out a box of cereal and ripped open its seal. Cheerios. Its crunch had filled her ears.

The only thing likely to explode in Old Chris's kitchen was the gas stove, but there was more to inhabiting it than she had anticipated. She wondered about asking Corinne over for coffee. Maybe working herself up to doing a pasta salad for the pair of them. They had seemed to hit it off in a small way—Corinne always asked about the beads, said she wanted to see some. She talked to

Frankie about her kids, who were in college now. Frankie talked a little about her old bead shop. "What do you think of us having a guest in, Old Chris?" she said aloud, "Make use of this big kitchen." Out in the chicken coop, she surveyed the workbench that stretched along most of the back wall, right under a wide window with an ocean view. No hiding from how far out in the ocean she was after all. She could see a lobster boat trailing a dozen sea gulls and heading out of sight. Frankie had screwed the torch stand into place and adjusted the clamps to set up her yellow gas canister. Half a dozen more clanked together in their cardboard box as she moved them under the bench with her foot.

The packed dirt floor was scattered with bits of glass that had flown, molten. Today her forearm was burned again from the hot specks. She had forgotten to roll down her shirtsleeves, forgotten that the molten glass would leave holes in her fleece pullover, forgotten the time. It was only when her back began to ache from standing that she paused. Frankie surveyed her morning's work. Some of the beads were scorched. And some of her mistakes came from the uneasiness she felt sometimes about the flame and its low roar. A little dangerous, she thought, just another way this whole enterprise is a little chancy.

"Nice to see this place in use," said a voice behind her. Startled, Frankie turned around, expecting to see Old Chris in her nail apron.

The tall frame silhouetted in the door was carrying a box under his arm. "I realized that you might be missing a few things in the kitchen, after all. I brought these down." He held up a tin colander. "Maybe this stuff will help out. Forgot a spatula, though. Next time."

Simon. Her landlord was a little older than she had expected. He had on a blue postal uniform polo shirt. Blue shirt, blue eyes. Kind face, all its creases upwardly mobile. So far he had just been a letter in the mail and a key left hanging on a hook to open a front door that hadn't been locked. She thought she might meet him at the post office when she went to pay her rent.

"Thanks," she said, reaching for the box. She could drain pasta now without losing it into the sink, she thought, looking at the colander. Frankie had never been grateful for kitchen utensils before, but here were the some of the gear works for getting through her meals after all—an egg beater, wooden spoons. She held up a sifter, letting its lever work rhythmically against its little disc of mesh, doing a little kitchen cha-cha sound. She had never used a sifter.

"How's this place treating you," he asked. "I hear from Corinne that you're settling in. Last time I was in this workshop, Old Chris was rebuilding some engine part for a lobster boat. The equipment has changed, I see."

Old Chris seemed to be able to do anything that needed doing. Frankie couldn't help wishing she could absorb her talents from the pages of *Hazzard's*. "Wish I could do that kind of thing. Do you know anyone around the island who fixes cars?" she asked. "I think I have something going on with my old vehicle."

"Not anymore. You have to call the Van Man—he comes over once a month with a van full of equipment—make an appointment with him for next time before all his one-hour slots are gone. He sets up in an old garage down by the wharf and lobster pound. If you get him over here on a special trip just for you, you have to pay his ferry both ways and the time he spends on it—and the time he waits for it once he finishes your job. If the car ever quits on you, I have a tow chain and we can get it to the wharf on Van Man day."

Frankie had actually hoped Simon would say to pop the hood and he could take a look at it. Maybe she was going to need to look through some of *Hazzard's* bulleted lists of car symptoms.

In the kitchen after Simon left, Frankie put her box of kitchenware on the bureau and grabbed the aloe from the tool drawer. Then she rooted around for something to eat. She was just considering whether or not she could actually turn a small bowl of softening apples into the apple bread that Old Chris had made in coffee cans when the phone rang for the first time in weeks. She looked at the calendar. Early May. Gabe must have received her letter. She cradled the phone between her shoulder and her ear and rinsed out the old coffee can that usually held the slender, foot-long stalks of glass caning, waiting for the inevitable on the other end of the line.

"What is the story with you, anyway," her brother exploded when she answered. "What are you doing on an island called Ile du Nord?"

Of course he would be upset: she had slipped by his big brother radar entirely, sold a business, changed zip codes. If she had told him earlier, all his cautions would have stopped her entirely. She had missed talking to him, rants and all—but even now she couldn't tell him all the details. "Making lunch—and burning beads," she answered. "Or, alternately, moving out of view of Luck Street. What are you up to?"

"This time you've really gone and done it!" He was yelling now. "Over the edge."

"I thought it was all trinkets and glorified beach glass," she answered.

"Oh, for God's sake, tell me you didn't take what I said to heart! You left because of what I said?"

"I was just having some bad days, Gabe."

"Having some bad days? So you sold everything? Francia, even you have to see that this time you've made a hell of a leap. So what now?"

Frankie had no answer. She wasn't going to tell him not to underestimate the power of the impulsive urge, or that her goal was Booth #373 at the late October show or that she was known as the bead artist on Ile du Nord. And then Frankie looked at cookbooks around her and improvised a ruse. "I'm writing a cookbook."

Gabe laughed, "Cookbook! All you do is open cans."

"Yes, but now I do it with style." A fat pamphlet called "Canning Do's and Canning Don'ts" caught Frankie's eye and she winged it: "It's going to be called *The All-Can Can-Do Cookbook*. For college students and new householders and all those in their first kitchens who want to enjoy food and maybe have people over for a meal." It actually began to seem like a wonderful idea. Cut and paste. Reinvent recipes. Old Chris had already given her lessons at this kind of thing. "I'm part way through the introduction," she lied, "and cooking up a storm."

Gabe was silent for a moment. This was a cookbook even he might buy. Then he said, "Frankie, how does this all work out?"

Frankie moved her imperfect bead back and forth on its linen cord, hoping it and days in her chicken coop studio and her big plans for the fall bead show would be protection enough for a new bead artist. She didn't really have an answer.

The day after Gabe's call, Frankie gave up on the chicken coop and the torch and let herself walk along Old Chris's shoreline for the first time since her arrival. The fog hadn't lifted all day. It had gone from wisps to a cloud that sat on Ile du Nord's granite shore. From out on the water came the husky thrum of a lobster boat. She walked through the mat of blonde and green grasses, over the lichened rocks, through a cluster of shore spruces and emerged at a shoreline of wet red granite. An old boathouse perched on the rocks above the retreating tide. A gull screeched from out in the mist, then wheeled into view and landed on the roof. Beside the small, weathered structure was a pile of ancient boards, lichened and gray, and amid them, a few rusty pieces of what she imagined had been an engine. Beyond this, rocks in craggy heaps sloped toward the water. In the crevices and along undersides of the wet boulders, sepia and gray periwinkles clustered; on more exposed slopes of rock there were constellations of tiny white barnacles, bright against the dark rock.

When Frankie got back to the house, she did not sketch beads in her notebook. Instead, she took out *Hazzard's New Engine Repair Guide* and looked for pictures of the engine parts she had found: a cylinder head with its combustion chambers exposed, a cam shaft cover. Then, she pulled out all her green and brown and bronze pencils and sketched seaweed and tiny sea shells in the margins around the crankcase and cylinder diagrams, trying to get the colors of rock and shell right, trying to capture what had caught her eye.

Gabe's questions always lingered: how did this all work out? The problem with beads was that they were small. Like marbles. Except that no one had ever prayed on a string of marbles. Or small like soup beans and pasta shapes—ingredients. The ideas that went into them seemed enormous, the urgency to create them, huge. But all there was to show was the brilliant rubble it took her so long to make. Perhaps creating an entire shore of them would be enough to quiet her doubt.

Later, she pulled out her old scraps of beading notes and diagrams made from art books and archeology texts and beading magazines and memory. In an antique store she had once found a knotted cord of opaque glass beads: each a different shade of unripe yellow, each with a different design of encased blue-green swirls, each made of molten glass a century before, probably more, on a small island in Venice. The dealer knew what he had and the price was more than she thought she could afford at the time, though she had wished since for the feel of them in her pocket. Old beads were accompaniment, the knowledge that someone had bent his head to the flame and watched them form. Now sketches of this old string of beads ornamented the edges *Hazzard's* chapter called "Connecting Rods," the designs she remembered swirling and eddying around each one.

And in the section called "Lighting Systems," she drew in a tiny bracelet she had taken notes on in a Chicago museum—fine bits of drilled coral twigs and minute eye beads for an eternity of luck. It had been removed from the wrist of a long-interred infant centuries before. The knotted string of beads lay in a display case, looking like jewelry on sale in the museum gift shop. Frankie wondered if that ancient baby hadn't still needed its tokens to accompany it from one world to the next. She started to transcribe other beads into the margins and open spaces in *Hazzard's*, until the old car repair manual began to look like a beading text.

In the weeks to come, when she looked out at the harbor while she worked or when she walked the shore or down to the ferry dock, Frankie realized she had made a miscalculation. She had once imagined the ocean and this island simply in terms of Lake Champlain—a glimpse of which she could catch from her bead shop—brilliant blues and whites on sunny days, the graphite tones of overcast days, waves lapping white, the tiny islands in the lake transformed from small green jewels to dark beads. Mountains, in tiers, rimmed the wide saucer of water, defining a shore. And across this expanse, the ferries going west to the Adirondacks slid past the ferries going east at mid-lake. But Ile du Nord was no island on a big lake. No easy refuge with a greater shore in sight. Remote.

Her uneasiness hadn't originated on a Maine island, though. The truth was that she used to wonder how it all worked out back in Vermont, too. That was what she had asked herself the day she had learned of Ile du Nord, the day she let the boyfriend—Marc—go. At lunchtime, she had headed down to Jake's for a crab roll, part of her almost daily routine at the bead shop. Mother of

Pearl's was up a steep flight of steps from Jake's Seafood, a tiny catering and take-out business that operated from what was mostly a loading dock with a narrow kitchen. She sometimes perched on a stool to talk to the owner while she waited for her lunch. As she headed down the alley and then up the loading dock steps, she heard, "Did that Frank guy come by for the crab roll he called in?"

"Hi," she said. "It's me. That Frank guy."

The new kid just looked up at her. No recognition. Somehow her frequency over his first few weeks had apparently not registered. Just a tiny component of her sense of not quite fitting where she was. Not quite out of place. Not quite in place.

"Mother's. I own Mother of Pearl's. Upstairs. I come here a lot."

At that moment, the owner came over from the cooler and waved the kid away.

Jake pulled down a take-out carton and motioned her to the stool. There were boxes of pasta in a row on the shelf at her shoulder as she sat down. "There are so many kinds," said Frankie, looking up at the twists of gemelli and spirals of fusilli and reaching for a box of midolini. The rattling contents looked like tiny seed beads. Pouring out a few, she started to bracelet a handful of the minute elliptical shapes in a circle on the counter.

"Different shapes, different recipes," said Jake. He grabbed the campenelli, shaking out the tubular flower shapes in his hand. "These little crevices really hold the sauce."

Thinking about the pasta in sauce made her hungrier. "Where are you from?" she asked, speaking up over the kitchen noises as Jake assembled the crab roll. Behind them an oven door slammed closed and a spatula clattered in the stainless steel sink. The background music was a blast of Irish punk. Frankie thought she remembered something about him once saying he had grown up on the ocean. She was feeling a lot like that Frank guy lately, a little invisible, wondering where she might fit in after all. She had arrived for college a dozen years ago from Ohio and, in some ways had simply never left. Most of her friends from that time had moved away. Lately, she had been thinking about setting up a bead studio and she had wondered if here was the place to do it after all. The whole notion of becoming a bead artist was probably a crazy scheme anyway.

"The coast of Maine, up beyond Mount Desert," Jake answered. "Remote. And there are islands there even more remote, way out in the ocean and connected only by ferry. One of the furthest is a gem called Ile du Nord. On a bad day, I tell myself that I'm giving up and heading to Ile du Nord to try my luck." He closed the lid on her carton and slid it in a bag. "How's business upstairs?"

Remembering Gabe's assessment, Frankie had reached for her lunch and answered, "Nearly successful. Business is very nearly successful."

And that afternoon she had written to the Ile du Nord postmaster. Did he know about a full-year island rental? Nothing fancy. A place for a bead artist to work on things. *Bead artist.* She had written it as if that were who she really was. And Simon St. John had written back that he himself had a place that had been vacant quite a while, but was habitable. Its chicken coop had been converted to a rough workshop. He offered it as a possible studio. She didn't decide to pick up the thread and write back to Simon to see if they could make arrangements until the night after the letter arrived.

She and Marc had gone down to a little bistro by the water for beer-battered trout.

He was talking about family plans, his mother's, for a big family brunch the coming weekend. Maple-baked peaches, three kinds of sweet breakfast rolls—including cranberry almond—and frittata. A spring tradition. Frankie didn't want to go, her mind on her new torch and the gold foil she had bought to incorporate into a bead, a big signature bead. And she still felt awkward with his family. If she had tried to explain to Gabe why she let the boyfriend go, there wouldn't have been a lot more to say than she had grown up eating cereal dry from the box while Marc's mother had served him maple-baked peaches at weekend family brunches.

And then, at dinner, Marc had begun to talk about can openers. That was what had finally done it, Frankie thought. The can openers. She had looked out at the mountains in view across the lake from the restaurant while he talked about his mother's collection of can openers. A ferry silently moved across the lake past a small island. Frankie had smiled at first, imagining her poking around flea markets for old gear-driven kitchenware—

but there were no garage sale can openers in this collection after all. The boyfriend's family was related to the can opener's inventor. They had one of the originals. 1825 patent seal. Museum quality.

Of course, thought Frankie.

"Did you know," asked Marc, "that cans were invented decades before the can opener? You had to use a hammer and chisel."

Cook with a hammer? Frankie imagined slamming open a can of chicken noodle soup. Watching her old standby explode appealed more than finishing her poached pear. She began, simply, to reveal her own life, in detail. About shared family meals being a matter of leaning her elbow on the counter while she ate yellow cling peaches from the can and talked to her brother as he checked the cupboard for Deviled Ham. About a kitchen full of appliances in virtually from-the-box condition, each one her mother's hope that she could plug a home life into an outlet and have it whir into existence on its own. This was a different story than the one he liked, the one about the pair of pharmaceutical doctorates who were her parents and the epidemiologist who was her brother, currently tracking strains of avian-borne flu in a state health lab. Both sets of stories were true, of course, but the one about the under-used kitchen and over-quiet house was more accurately the story of her growing up.

"My mother was into can openers, too." Frankie said, leaning forward a little over her untouched dessert, "to open cans of cream of mushroom soup to make that French fried onion ring and green bean casserole. We had chicken noodle soup every day for one entire summer, my brother and I. Our sandbox was outfitted with spray-painted cans for playing mud pies and castles. The little orange tuna cans were my favorite."

We come from different worlds, she had said to herself, and I've had a bad day. She watched Marc's face shift. A little disclosure, a little shift in emphasis. And that was all it took to begin their goodbye. That and backing out of another event for the sake of her new bead torch. Beads took a lot of time—and since Mother of Pearl's was open six days a week, there wasn't much of that. She could be a jewelry maker in the quiet times at the shop, but she couldn't be a bead artist with her torch turning glass canes molten in between customers. Frankie had unintentionally lost track of the time more than once while she taught herself to flamework beads. And she had scrapped or postponed their plans more than once to work on beads, including a weekend with his family. That cancellation had become one of the legends of their relationship. Proficiency at the torch didn't come with limited bits of time and before Ile du Nord, that's all she had had to give it.

He had asked at dinner if she were going to stand his folks up again for an afternoon's play. Frankie knew that calling it an afternoon's play had been angry talk, but it still stung. Ordinarily, Marc had thought her beads accomplished—his word for them. Ordinarily, he was happy with her talents. She created a bracelet as a birthday gift for his sister: silver toggle, Tibetan beads.

And now she and her trinkets—Gabe's word—and baubles had moved to Ile du Nord. Hadn't the boyfriend called them baubles? Maybe not. Perhaps remembering things that way was an act of ventriloquism, making the old boyfriend voice her own worries. Maybe the misgivings were all her own—after all, an afternoon's work wouldn't even fill a pocket. Here was the familiar anxiety—that what she loved best was trivial. Whatever Marc had said, maybe the fear that it would all remain small and rattling—her life like the sound of remnant pasta in a cardboard box—was all hers. And that uneasiness had followed her to Ile du Nord after all.

And now, here on the island, there had been a string of days that had been nothing like nearly successful. Gabe's phone call had given her the blues. On the beach, she had found the remains of a dead baby seal, turned to a kind of leather, looking like a child's empty pajamas, its flippers like the feet in nighttime sleepers. Later, she decided to respond to the call for volunteers to help renovate the library. She had shown up to build bookshelves, her tool tote with her, only to have Simon's cousin Lennie and some of the others tell her they had enough help. On her way back home, she wondered if she had found a way to offend someone already. The car gave a little lurch as she eased around the corner to Quarry Road and then accelerated. Or tried to. A pause. Not really a sputter. Like it couldn't catch its breath. Something was wrong and the only mechanic she knew of on the island was dead. At the turn-off, near the house with the lobster boat up on jack stands, the little hatchback paused again, this time a bigger lurch, like it had run out of gas or air or both. Not that she couldn't sympathize, just that she didn't know how to fix it.

At dinnertime, Frankie flipped *Hazzard's* open to the table of contents, which was set up alphabetically. Under "L" there was nothing listed for "lurch," but there were lots of entries under "Lubrication." After the last one, which had something to do with crankcases and pumps, she found an entry penned in: *Lucky's Casserole, p. 317.* She really didn't care what she cooked. She had car trouble, money worries and she felt awkward with the islanders. And tonight she was ready to chisel open any can at random or swim back to the mainland. She started flipping her way through the manual toward the casserole recipe.

Hazzard's revealed itself in layers. She saw something new in it every time she opened it. Next to pictures of a generator, there was a note that read: *alternator light flickering—pulley worn—get Lennie the belt the next size down from what the parts book calls for.*

Frankie turned to the inside of the back cover, sliding some folded newspaper clippings into place when they slipped out. There was the crossed-out part number for Lennie's Jeep and a list of phone numbers—starting with Simon's. So that's who Old Chris would call first, she thought, realizing that would be her choice, too. Then came The Island Store and auto parts places in Ellsworth. And a number for Corinne and one for Lennie. There were two numbers listed for a Terrance, both crossed out. There was another number, one with another name she didn't recognize. Nicky Z. A Maine number, but not Ile du Nord. No entry for the Maggie of the Southwinds recipe.

Then came a series of long distance numbers. Before seeing these numbers, it had never occurred to her that Old Chris might have connections off the island. What would she learn if she called any of these, she wondered. On impulse, Frankie keyed the first of them. Boston. A medical center. What was the story, she asked herself, as she apologized and hung up. Did Old Chris go there? Or her husband? Was the story so sad the islanders didn't want to talk about it?

Had Old Chris been married? The kitchen had a single person's feel to it. There weren't two complete place settings of anything that matched and there was only one white coffee mug.

Frankie turned back to page 317.

Pasted over the first page of Chapter 16, "Fuel Feed Systems," was the recipe called *Lucky's Casserole*. Underneath the recipe's name, Old Chris had inked *You have many chances to get this right, but maybe not as many as it takes.* The ingredients list included a can of soup—*whatever you can find*—*a cup or two of noodles or rice, cooked or uncooked, if you have it. A can of vegetables or a can of anything else. Whatever you put in this will disappear. Bake until you remember to take it out.* And then it said, *This recipe will get you by, if you're lucky.*

It sounded a lot like the dinner she had considered putting together. Instead, Frankie thumbed her way back to page 25 and, scanned the ingredients of the recipe she found there. Time for a quick trip to the Island Store. "How did you manage life alone on Ile du Nord, Old Chris?" She heard herself asking the question aloud.

At the Island Store, an exiting trio of kids and their mother were unwrapping ice cream treats as Frankie made her way in. A month ago, ice cream on a stick could have been a quick, temporary solution to a mealtime dilemma, but even that easy answer didn't dissuade Frankie. Corinne's husband, Jacko, was the one at the register as she put down a carton of eggs and a package of yeast. "How's life out on Quarry Road?" he asked.

"Not bad," she said, "But I admire Old Chris and her ability to make do more and more. She must have been a remarkable woman."

"Woman? Hey, Corinne, Frankie here says she thinks Old Chris must have been a remarkable woman," said Jacko.

Lennie and his wife, Elizabeth, were there and they laughed aloud. The pair of them looked like members of the same team, about the same height and stocky stature and wearing very similar putty-colored warm-up jackets. Jacko pulled down the photo of the Ile du Nord ferry on its first run. In the photo were all the Ile du Nord men who had had a hand in building the dock and terminal.

"That's me and Simon," said Lennie, leaning in and pointing.

Jacko tapped the image of a powerful-looking man in a dark knit cap: "And this is Old Chris St. John. Just back from the Navy and Korea. He was in charge of the building project."

Of course, thought Frankie, this old story. Francia, Frankie,

2011 Press 53 Open Awards

that Frank guy. The girl occasionally assigned to boys' gym classes in school. How did I miss this piece, she wondered.

"And this," said Jacko, indicating the young man standing next to Frankie's Quarry Road roommate, "is Young Chris. Old Chris was a year old when another couple on the island named their infant Chris, too. Eventually, Young Chris moved to the mainland, but the name Old Chris stuck. His brother said there was never a time when the name Old Chris didn't fit him. Actually, his brother's name for him was Old Piss."

"Mine, too," said Lennie.

Frankie turned to look at him as she asked, "Brother?"

Corinne put her finger on the glass over the other St. John in the picture. "Terrance. 'Lucky' they called him. 'Lucky there are no bars or jails on Ile du Nord or he'd be in one or the other of them all the time,' they used to say. But I guess he wasn't so lucky in the end."

"Stole my jeep once," said Lennie, "buried it in the muck up to the axles."

"Was Old Chris a lobsterman?" Frankie asked, taking the photo in her hands.

"No—builder mostly, mechanic by default—fixing people's boat engines and truck mufflers just because he was pretty good at it and he was always being asked. Old Chris wanted nothing to do with the ocean. And what's all this?" asked Corinne, gesturing at ingredients that clearly went beyond warming and assembly.

"Poor Woman's Soup," said Frankie, distracted and looking at the photograph. Old Chris, the Queen of the Kitchen with her car repair manual full of recipes. The woman whose nail apron she wore when she made beads or supper or walked on the beach collecting shells. Old Chris—her Old Chris—had fixed dinners and fixed cars on Ile du Nord and convinced Frankie that she could get by on Quarry Road.

And she and Old Chris had shared *Hazzard's*. The battered manual had kept both of them fed and now it held Frankie's bead sketches—margin after margin of the thin pages in the thick book rendered ornate with remembered images and planned beads and beads reinterpreted from clippings she had stashed before she arrived in the island. She had talked to Old

Chris out loud and in her head, trying to channel the inventive and durable energy of the woman who had managed to pull this place off. The woman who taught her an apple bread she could bake in coffee cans. Gone. *How do I get used to this?* Frankie wondered as she started to gather her things. And then Corinne fastened on her.

"Poor Woman's Soup! There is no such recipe. That was Old Chris's soup. There were only ever three people in the world who knew about that—me and Old Chris and the dying woman he made it for. You don't know anything about Old Chris—or Maggie!"

Maggie's recipe, thought Frankie. The Boston numbers.

"Why did you choose here to do your beads, anyway," interjected Elizabeth. Lennie's querulous wife had never seemed to warm to Frankie the few times circumstances had brought them together. What had she done to offend the home team?

"Here to set up a studio," she began.

Corinne interrupted, saying, "I'd like to hear what Old Chris would think of a bead artist staying at his place."

Corinne had always been so friendly. Frankie wondered what she had managed to screw up.

"And what would any of us actually ask Old Chris if we had the chance to talk to him again, I wonder," said a new voice, cutting through the interrogation as Simon came through the screen door. Frankie made no replies. She slipped past Simon and was gone before there was an answer to his question.

Simon found Frankie at Spruceside Cemetery, up on the knoll just off Quarry Road. Three gravestones had already claimed her attention by the time he arrived. Maggie St. John, wife of Christopher, dead too young, nearly as young as Lucky. The word Beloved inscribed on her stone. And two cenotaphs. Lucky's, whose stone read Terrance "Lucky" St. John, followed by "Lost on the Ocean." And Christopher St. John's. It, too, read "Lost on the Ocean." A little row of periwinkles, sun-bleached an almost perfect white, lined his granite marker. Frankie was sitting crossed-legged on the grass.

Simon squatted down beside her and said, "We take some getting used to."

"Why do they mind that I'm staying at Old Chris's place? Because Lennie thought his son could have it?"

"Well, you've got them all a little unnerved. Just the fact that there are lights on in the house after all this time—it's been years. You and Old Chris have the only place on the point. Everyone along the harbor road can see the house lit up in the dark and it's brought back talk of Old Chris. And then there's your clothesline. Lennie nearly drove into a tree when he came around the bend saw it the first time."

"My clothesline?"

"Old Chris used that same thick flamingo pink electric wire to string out his laundry. And wore battered Carhartts, just like yours, when he worked on boats. Brown workpants flapping on the line were like flying Old Chris's flag. Elizabeth is still sure you do it just to spook us."

Frankie lay back in the grass, trying to take it all in. "Why wasn't Lucky so lucky?" she asked. "How did he end up lost on the ocean?"

"Drowned. And the day before he died, he and Old Chris had it out again on the St. John dock. Lucky trying to get him to fix his boat on the cheap and go fishing with him. I was up at the house with Maggie and we heard Lucky hollering 'What in hell is your problem, Old Piss, just back-flush it with gasoline!' And Old Chris yelled back something about Lucky getting himself over to the mainland to buy the damn parts. Then Lucky started to taunt him about not fishing."

"Why didn't he fish?" she asked.

"He lobstered a little as a teenager. Had plans for a fishing boat, maybe, after the Navy. When he got back from Korea, though, he just wasn't interested."

"So he didn't go out with Lucky that day?"

"Nope. Old Chris came back to the house sputtering because he'd gotten a mouthful of stale gasoline from blowing grit out of Lucky's fuel filter. Said he'd about had it, that he wouldn't keep fixing Lucky's boat, much less stern on it. Maggie took Lucky's side. For all his angry bluster, though, Chris always kept Lucky going."

"But not this time?"

"Chris did the best he could without the new parts that afternoon, but the boat really was in sorry shape. They had dropped an old car engine in it, straight from a wreck. It always ran hot and nothing to be done about it. The weather was foul that next day—nobody else on the water and for good reason. Lucky insisted on going—said he'd be fine. Old Chris showed up on the dock with his gear on that morning after all, like Lucky knew he would. But in a few minutes, Old Chris was back in his own kitchen, pulling off his boots—in the end, Lucky wouldn't let him go out that day."

"Why do you suppose he refused the help after all?"

"Even Lucky must have known how crazy it was to go out. I like to think he didn't want to risk both his brother and his boat."

"What happened when he didn't come back?"

"Ile du Nord never forgave Old Chris."

"Forgive him for what? Not going out with Lucky?"

"Well, for not going out with him or for not preventing him from going. Old Chris had always been pretty independent, but he came back from the Navy remote, even harder to know. Angry, sometimes. He avoided anything that brought him out on the ocean and that meant he refused to go lobstering with the little brother who had become famous for his chancy ways. Ile du Nord didn't know what to make of him and they didn't know what to do about Lucky."

"What was Lucky's problem?"

"Who knows," Simon shrugged, "but Old Chris spent a lifetime pulling him out of scrapes. Things got worse while Old Chris was in the service. We thought he'd calm down a bit if Old Chris would just partner with him. Maybe pay some of his bills. Folks felt that when Old Chris came home from Korea he just left the rest of the island to cope with Lucky."

"Did you?"

"Maybe a little. But no net was going to catch Lucky. After he drowned, though, the islanders were pretty distant with Old Chris. And he and Lennie never got along."

"Was Corinne distant with him?" asked Frankie. She remembered the list of phone numbers in *Hazzard's*. "Were you?"

"No," said Simon, "but I had kids at home still and I had a job and ran a few lobster traps. I was busy." Then he added, "Maybe more busy than I had to be. And Corinne—you need to understand something about Old Chris and Corinne."

"What about them? Weren't they friends?" And then it dawned on Frankie. They had been more than friends. "Does everyone know?" she asked.

"Just me, I'm sure," said Simon. "She was married. It was before Jacko fell and hurt his leg working for the power company on the mainland. Before they expanded the store. Maggie died in the fall—maybe Old Chris and Corinne were together over a winter, maybe part of a spring. And then no more. I'm telling you because she's having to share him with you now, in a way, and having to remember. She seems to like you, even if today was a little ragged. Be good to her." The old postmaster put his hands on his knees and rose slowly from the grass. "It's been a long time since Old Chris died," he said. "I thought we were up to the idea of someone living there again. Maybe I was wrong."

"So how did Old Chris die?" asked Frankie, pointing at the lichened inscription as she stood up with him, trying to take in what she had learned. "How did he end up lost on the ocean, too?"

"Another day," said Simon. "I've done enough remembering for now." He nodded his head toward the stone in acknowledgment and waved back at Frankie without turning around as he walked away across the grass and pine needles.

On the way home, the car lurched as she tried to pull away from the stop sign at the turn onto the hill that led to Quarry Road. "Intake, compression," she chanted to herself, like a mantra for all battered island vehicles, "power, exhaust." She turned off the ignition and tried again. "Intake, intake, intake!" she shouted, fears of the Van Man looming, inevitable. If it quit here, she didn't even have anyone to call to help her out. They had all been back at the store. The wagon's engine caught, stumbled forward and quit—but by now they—she and the car—were in the middle of the intersection. She cramped the steering wheel till they were aimed down the incline and let it slowly start to roll till they were poised at the steepest part of the hill. She slid the clutch in and let the car gather speed—and, half way down the hill, she popped the clutch. The car coughed and then engaged, roaring around the curve a little fast for the deepness of the bend but she and the car were going on adrenalin now. "What do I do now, Old Chris?" she asked aloud, "have a go at this on my own or call the Van Man?" Just pulling into her driveway felt like a victory.

Inside, she grabbed *Hazzard's* and flipped back to "Fuel Feed Systems" and Lucky's Casserole. "Troubles and Remedies," began page 520 and on the opposite page was a cut-away view of a fuel pump. Written in the margin was a part number, *1749A, gas filter.* She scanned the bulleted list of symptoms: engine hesitation, rough idle, poor low-speed performance, stop and start problem, failure to turn over—and, of course, simply quitting in the middle of the road, thought Frankie. There was the diagram for removing the fuel filter—it looked like a small soup can.

Frankie did everything the old engine guide said and then she sat on her front steps with it beside her and the hood of the car propped open. An array of Old Chris's wrenches from the bottom drawer of the kitchen bureau were lined up on the fender. And she was pungent with the gas that had sprayed when she had released the fuel filter from its hoses. The manual hadn't mentioned that. She was staring at the note Old Chris had written in ink up the side of the margin: *The only way to be sure is to remove the filter and try to blow through it. Mind the gasoline.*

Mind the gasoline, thought Frankie, and she tried to be careful, but Old Chris hadn't fully explained the whole technique for this procedure. She felt the fumes, sharp, in her nose and she felt the grit in her mouth and spat. The burn of the gas on her lips and tongue was intense and then residual.

And the filter had failed the test. Too clogged to blow through. The manual said to open it and rinse the interior screen with gasoline, but this thing looked permanently sealed. There were clamps and a hose that had split when she worked it off lying on the ground near her car. Her engine had shed some pieces and reassembly at this point was improbable unless Old Chris materialized out of the incoming fog with a fuel filter in his pocket. Confronted with an ailing car and an old car manual that didn't make full disclosure, she packed up her tools. Time for a shower. Time for a meal.

In the kitchen, Frankie cleared a space, shoving jars of new beads and a stack of bills aside on the counter, and opened

Hazzard's to page 25 and the recipes for Poor Woman's Soup and Southwinds. Frankie pulled open the top drawer of the scorched bureau, shifted aside the gas nozzle and grabbed her slicing knife. Medallions of carrots strung themselves out across her counter "So this was your first recipe, old friend," she said aloud. "This time we're at it together for real." Golden oil simmered in the dented pot. She was damp and still smelled faintly of gasoline and her mouth still burned, but she was hungry.

Later, when the Southwinds bobbed up in the hot oil, Frankie searched for a slotted spoon to ladle them out and then gave up, settling for pinioning the hot golden rolls with the long thin screwdriver. They broke open to a snowy white.

Stroke 3: Power

In the morning, Frankie found an old bicycle, fixed speed, leaning against her car. Simon. There was no real need to stray far from Quarry Road, she thought. She would think about the car later. The bike was an answer for a while. She let the hood she had forgotten to close the day before slam down. Time to think about beads and not get distracted by fuel filters. Time for the chicken coop.

Back in her old neighborhood, Frankie could shut out the noises of Luck Street as she worked—the kids, the cars, the occasional sirens at night. Here, though, she let it all in. There was the chime of the buoy in the harbor. The sound of its rocking and rebalancing in the waves and tide was a background sound that filtered into her very house. From the tops of spruces in the surrounding field and woods, the crows pumped their glistening black heads as they blasted the air with their cawing. The gulls shrieked and called. There was the deepening and waning thrum of lobster boats headed in and out of the harbor. Sometimes she heard music from a radio on one of the boats, loud classic rock and local ads getting airtime across the water.

And there was the light. On the point where some ancient St. John had built this wood frame house, the wash of light through the many windows was admitted on all sides. She waited for the best light to work on the most ambitious beads and avoided the times the dazzle of sun on the ocean and the flood of light through the studio window left her workbench back-lit. In that light, the flame tip dangerously disappeared from view.

With the sounds and the light, the house pulled in weather at every turn. There were times on the island when the changes of temperature and sky seemed to encompass three seasons in a single day. When the damp filled the place on Quarry Road late on a wet day, apple bread, hot, was the only cure. On very chilly days she had to be patient introducing the cold glass canes to the flame or they would shatter. She could not be here and ignore these elements that defined her days.

Even more impossible to ignore than the weather were the colors, especially the greens—the retreating tide revealed colors that were saturated and, in the frequent mist, often glossy and nearly luminous, especially on overcast days. The ocean itself was a somber green, and the waves defined themselves in the silvered light that filtered through the mist. She had a sense that she had never seen green like this—there was the amber-green of moss and the gray-green of lichens and the bronze-green of rockweed. There was the wet lime green of seaweed on the beach.

Green, though, was just the beginning of it. Rain and fog transformed landscape and color and she found herself exploring the rocky shoreline. For her, the blue of this island was the rich deep lapis blue of the mussels that emerged at low tide below the exposed rocks. It was the indigo-violet of shells caught in polished fragments in the wet red rock crevices near Old Chris's house. Their colors were acute and saturated on wet days, surprising her each time with their intensity. The color of rust took on dimension. It streaked the periwinkle shells she gathered by the handful in her nail apron. In the spruces close to shore, the wet cones were rusty against the bright lime of the branch tips. Damp red-orange spruce needles carpeted the path to the boathouse. Even the blonde grasses purpled and grew russet at the tip in the field between her house and woods. The long windows of the house often blackened to reflective mirrors and sometimes on her approach she would catch her reflection, her own rusty red hair the color of what she now saw around her.

Of all her answers to the loneliness she had brought with her, the best rescues were the colors on a wet day and *Hazzard's* manual.

She had arrived with a small collection of beads of her own, inspiration and talismans. Years ago, before she even became a beader, she had bought a short string of very old amber beads—some of them translucent and some of them cloudy—and had found a single extraordinary etched carnelian bead at a flea market. Marc had given her a half a dozen Neolithic agate beads when he came back after traveling to a conference. He had apologized when he gave them to her, saying that they seemed so imperfect. He had looked for mosaic glass. Instead, the gift had touched her. To line the small, flint-drilled discs up in a row on the window sill was to feel as though she were up to something that was so deeply human that perhaps she didn't have to explain it to herself.

Besides her small cache of ancient beads, she had brought bead sketches of what were meant to be signature beads on their own cord or silver strand, single beads built in patient layers over the length of whole afternoons. Her first one—the one she had skipped brunch for, the one that had triggered the goodbyes with Marc—was around her neck. It wasn't a perfect sphere, though the swirls of gold foil inside disguised that—and it had minute air bubbles that could only be seen on the closest inspection. The plan had been to create a series of knockout, virtuoso beads for the bead show—ones that could command fifty or one hundred dollars apiece. These were beads that could emerge from torch and kiln as magic as amulets—or as ordinary as plunkers and dresser pulls.

Since she had been here, though, *Hazzard's* margins filled with other things. At home, at night, she would sketch necklaces that used the unexpected colors that surrounded her: multiple strands of seed beads in wet granite red, strung with torch-made beads in lapis and indigo. Or she would draw coils of waxed green linen with ivory-white beads streaked in rust and caught in the twisted strands.

In the daytime, she would rest her elbows on the workbench and hold rods of glass in a pencil grip in the flame, watching them blaze yellow and the glass go molten orange and begin to move like thick honey. The ivory cane seemed to flow the most quickly and the green cane seemed to melt the most slowly as she patiently wound it on the metal rod, the world briefly as small and focused as the glass and the flame. She attuned herself to the distinct way each color met the torch and to the ways that colors combined and at night dreamed that her fingertips could shoot a blue flame that thinned as it reached out.

And instead of creating perfect single beads, she would spend whole afternoons trying to make a dozen small streaked beads that caught the eye the way shells would, evoking an impression without a trace of mimicry. Beads different from each other and identical to each other in the same ways these small shells and bits of smoothed granite beach gravel were.

In the early morning on Ile du Nord, the low light gave the water and sky—and even the spruce hillside of the harbor she faced from a distance—a muted quality. The houses on the steep rise above the shore stood out, bright white in the first sun. Clustered and grouped, the houses gleamed briefly like sprays of white barnacles exposed on dark rock at low tide. Anchored here, caught here. The dazzle of this all held in constellation lasted just for the brief moments as the early sun shot low over the water, and then the sun would rise a degree or two and the houses would become simply white and yellow and gray homes in a colorful landscape of spruce and docks and anchored lobster boats. At those early moments of her day, Frankie would be pierced, briefly, by a sense of them all, the people who lived here. And that was it, just a sense, somehow, of them all, held here.

She began to make tiny white bicone beads that evoked for her both barnacles and houses. These she did not encase in the transparent glass that she used to keep the luminous quality of wet mussel shell or wet granite. Wet or dry, barnacles always seemed a flat, baked white. She tried to preserve some of that quality in her beads, which she scored around the holes at each end while the glass was still molten, ridging both sides of each bead in a way that recalled the pie crust edges of the small crustaceans whose caught collective beauty she was trying to convey.

Sometimes, as the tide was going out, she would listen to the rattle of shells and small stones drawn back toward the ocean in the surge and retreat of waves. Maybe that was the sound track of what she did. Not the sound of pasta in its box. The sound of something old washed back in its ancient element.

As well as the beading was going, there was no getting around the fact that there was nothing much left in the fridge but eggs: she was running out of ingredients. Out on her bike—Simon's now-grown-and-gone daughter's bike—she had discovered that nearly everyone on Ile du Nord kept chickens and sold eggs—or that at least two neighbors did. Her pockets always had a boiled egg or two for lunch while she was working in her studio. No need to even break pace and go inside for lunch. Her time away from The Island Store had become another master class in making do.

On a bike ride, she had even found a stretch of beach where the stones sorted themselves out in bands of the same size, all of them granite and egg-shaped. In the lower band, the stone eggs were enormous, dinosaur scale. When she came home, she had pockets full of small speckled eggs from the upper reaches of beach where the rockweed was tangled with gull feathers and twists of orange rope and broken urchin shells, but no prospects of much beyond scrambled eggs for dinner. She lined the stones up on the window sill and opened *Hazzard's* to make sketches for beads—ovate shapes in natural tones of sepia and gray, thinly encased in clear molten glass to look always damp from a receding tide. Eggs had become answers.

And today they looked like her only answers. What now? She had the eggs—and a little flour, but not enough to make anything she had learned. And she was still looking for a solution for something to eat that didn't involve The Island Store. The avoidance had some natural limits, but she would rather save this day for beading and plunge into the island's social adventures later. What wisdom did the old Navy man have for how she fed herself today?

This was a test for *Hazzard's*, one it was destined to fail. She had skimmed past crêpes any number of times, unwilling to try a recipe whose name required a diacritical mark. She paused just to mock it and her culinary abilities. But here it was – the recipe she had ingredients for. A little flour, the last of her milk, eggs. Once she mixed it, she was a little surprised by the thin batter, skeptical that it could yield a meal—but if it had asked for more of anything but eggs, she wouldn't have had enough to complete it. She'd used Simon's sifter, batting its sides to shake the white dust free, watching it cone up in the bowl.

Old Chris had drawn a sketch of where to set the heat dial for the gas flame. The heat floated the eggy film on the hot metal of the pan. How could something so insubstantial feed hunger, thought Frankie. The insubstantial fluid became something gossamer-like, veil-like. The crêpe pulled away from the pan and its shape, like a slightly distorted Ile du Nord, began to take on an edge that seemed to hover above the pan, rippling gently.

Flip, said the recipe. Flip? There was no spatula in the entire kitchen and the sharp edge of the putty knife might tear this miracle. She reached out with her hand and pinched an edge carefully, then more confidently, as the heat of the resilient little island nearly, but didn't, burn her fingertips. And, gently, she turned it over with her fingers.

When the crêpe was done, Frankie folded it into a triangle and dipped it into the sugar bowl. The edges sparkled, crystalline. The folded crêpe felt like nothing she had ever touched, certainly not like a bready thing or like a tiny pancake. She ate it in four bites, but a leisurely four bites—impossible not to stop and think about how good it felt to eat it. She paused, considered the tender thing in her mouth, the view out the window, the recipe in the automotive guide. An egg or two, some coffee scoops of flour. It will all make sense in the end. Just follow the directions, said the recipe and Old Chris was right again. She finished the batter, peeling the last crêpe off the pan with her fingers and tried to read the topography of the island in the whorls of faint brown across its surface. She felt fed. There was almost always enough in her kitchen to make crêpes. The recipe was so good, it was a shame not to share it: she wanted to make this for someone. What an odd impulse, she thought. But there was no one on the island she could make crêpes for. And here was the unexpected part of this recipe, the joy of feeding herself and the pinch of having no one to it cook for.

The weeks of uneasiness started to burn off on her resumed visits to The Island Store. Her fridge and cupboards were full—she had developed a small hoarder's habit for stashing staples she might need in an emergency—an alienated store owner, supplies that didn't reach the island one week—that she assumed was an island trait. *Hazzard's* was propped open on the counter and Frankie taped in a catalogue picture of the new bead maker's torch she wanted. She wrote the item number and the 800 number of the supplier in the margin of the book. The key to working with the torch she used now was patience, but she wanted a little more heat. A white flame. Hot enough that the molten glass stayed true and clear in any color. Her uneasiness about the yet hotter flame, as much as cost, kept her from ordering the torch. She understood the flame when it licked yellow around the melting glass, but it thinned to invisibility at the tip. It was in this nearly imperceptible zenith of flame, where she had to rely on sensing it rather than seeing it, that she was sometimes uncomfortable.

The torch wasn't her most pressing problem, though. It was glass caning. And money. She was not only a little short of a full year's rent here, but the glass cane she had brought with her didn't reflect anything she wanted to do now. One morning she gathered up her beader's supply catalogue and a list of the colors of glass she needed to buy and opened *Hazzard's* to "Piston Rings." These pages were now designated for accounts: columns and categories of expenses and assets—mostly expenses—laid out on taped-in graph paper. Adding it twice didn't seemed to solve anything. Subdividing her weekly living allowances into smaller units bought her only enough for a small order of glass. She needed greens particularly and indigo and more linen cord. Lennie's wife seemed to be in charge of things at the library— would she let Frankie use the library a night a week to offer a class? Would people on the island scoop up their jelly jars of collected beach glass and bring them to a found-art jewelry workshop?

Her unexpected asset was a stash of single rods that had come as freebies with her last order. They were in colors she never thought she would use: hot pink, electric green, neon orange. Now Frankie watched the lobster floats across the harbor and in front of her door ride the surface of the water in these same neon hues, their own improbable visual treat. At first, experimenting with the glass at the end of a day's work, she would make a few beads with this glass she had nearly thrown away. Then, she began to string these near-fluorescent beads on subdued green linen, each knotted in place in wide irregular intervals with small silver beads from her original cache, multiple strands caught and clasped in a small silver cone at each end. These were not crafted to imitate lobster floats, but when she looked at them strung on their fine cords, she heard in her mind the fast return, big-waked, of Toomey's fishing boat.

The screen door rattled in its frame and Frankie looked up from *Hazzard's* to see Corinne knocking. Closing the book and sliding it off to the side of the counter past a bowl with remnant batter and a mound of curling apple peels, she got up to let her in.

"Well," Corinne said through the wire mesh, "do you think we've patched things up, you and I?"

"Of course we have," Frankie said, flipping the eyehook.

"What are you baking?" asked Corinne, checking out the kitchen as she slipped through the door.

"Fixing apple bread again."

"Fixing? That's what Old Chris called cooking—like it was a broken thing he had to take care of."

Frankie bent to light the oven and swore as the pilot light went out for the second time. There's technique to every damn thing I try here, she thought, lighting another match.

"I haven't been here for a long time," Corinne said, picking up the mason jars along the top of the bureau: clear glass pints filled with bits of sea-smoothed mollusk shell all the same size, sepia-gray granite egg-stones and periwinkles chosen for their ocean-bleached whiteness. "Old Chris always kept a handful of these in his pocket," she said holding the last one up, "mixed with the odd hex nut or washer or two."

The periwinkles. "You're the one who put the shells on his stone," said Frankie.

"I'm the one," said Corinne finding a chair. "Look, Frankie, I'm here with an offer. Cassie Fontaine, the town clerk, passed away in a hospital on the mainland just before you arrived. No one on the island really wants the job. Want to fill out her term? Part-time. Nuisance work, really. Not much pay." Corinne slid a key toward her.

"I'm only here for a year," said Frankie, wondering at her turn of luck.

"We'll take a year," Corinne said. On the table there were several cans filled with Frankie's beading mistakes. Corinne poured some into her hand. "For bead soup?" she asked.

"Trial and error with the beads," said Frankie. "Mostly error." She managed to successfully ignite the oven. "I'll give it a go," she said, reaching for the key to the little office in the back of the library.

"Great," said Corinne. "You know, Maggie was a wonderful cook in spite of that stove. She made a legendary lemon meringue pie. People used to line up for it at the library's annual island dinner. Then, the summer or two she was too sick to do it, Old Chris took over. Lemon filling the color of sunsets. Huge crests of meringue six inches high." Corinne lined up three slightly misshapen barnacle beads. "Beautiful," she said.

"Keep them," said Frankie.

"You know," said Corinne, "I didn't think it would be so hard to see the lights on up here again." She drew a long leg up under her chin as she sat and rested her chin on her blue-jeaned knee. Then she asked, "What did Simon tell you?"

"Almost nothing, except to let me know there was something to tell. And to tell me to be good to you."

"Sounds like Simon. He was the only one who knew. Maybe I'm not sorry someone else knows after all this time."

"Did you and Old Chris cook together?"

"I'd come over to help out so much before Maggie died, it seemed ordinary enough to come check in on him afterwards. He didn't even have much of any cookware left. Did Simon tell you that the morning Maggie was buried, he loaded all her cookware into an old boat tarpaulin and hauled it out to the buoy where the ferry turns and dumped it? Half the town saw him rowing out in his suit. An hour later, he stood in the cemetery, wet to the knee, as she was lowered into the grave. I don't think anyone got over the sight of him that day. They thought he was crazy. Or disrespectful."

"Simon didn't fill me in," Frankie said, thinking of the contents of her kitchen and the spatula that she had looked for that was now at the bottom of the ocean.

"Couldn't bear the thought of meals without her—that's what he said. I kept him company for a few months after she died. Let him cook for me. Didn't realize we would be reading cookbooks in bed."

What recipes in *Hazzard's* had the old widower tried out on Corinne, Frankie wondered as she listened to her. Her kids had just started to go to high school off-island during the week back then and Jacko still had his job with the power company. And, maybe, thought Frankie, Corinne was feeling just then like she needed more than the short aisles of The Island Store.

"All that winter," Corinne was saying, "And, at the end of spring, the kids ready to move back home full-time for the summer, he sent me away. It seemed for the best."

Sent away. On an island this small.

"Stay a while," said Frankie, "the apple cake is best warm."

That night, remembering Old Chris and his pockets, Frankie emptied her own pockets of their habitual talismans—half a dozen burned beads, three tiny granite eggs, her own small stash of shells and a bit of beach glass that might once have been the top of a bottle but was now a perfect thick ring of weathered blue-green glass—and spread them out on the nightstand. Not all beading gathered itself on a string.

When it was time to go to work, Frankie was pretty sure that the island didn't stand on too much ceremony over what their town clerks wore in their tiny library office, but she was giving the choice some attention. She chose the batik wrap-around skirt that had been her favorite to wear at the bead shop. The real choice was the jewelry. The bead on its cord was almost a companion now—but she wanted a bracelet, too, or another necklace. A few strands of something.

Adornment, accompaniment. As she held up the possibilities, she remembered an elderly woman who came into her shop with a small crowd of granddaughters or nieces—all given the go-ahead to grab beader's layout trays and create necklaces of their own. And once the girls got underway—the smallest refusing assistance, two older girls in deep collaboration, the fourth girl heading directly for turquoise—their elderly mentor put on her reading glasses and took a tray of her own, taking a barrette from her pocket and twisting her hair behind her head like she were going to work in earnest. She might have been eighty, Frankie guessed, and still fairly easy in her old bones. Frankie watched her choose beads, consider shapes, creating a pattern in the bead tray's channel. What she did was no different than what her small swarm of girls were doing: she wasn't creating an old woman's necklace, she was seeking to ornament herself as she had always done—as if the woman who wanted to adorn her neck was neither young nor old, simply the woman who had looked out at the world from those same eyes for decades. Adornment was an ancient way of meeting the world or meeting one's self. Stringing beads was time travel.

The July meeting of Ile du Nord's Library Association was held a few weeks later in its half-renovated library and the latest topic was their finances: there wasn't enough money to complete the building project. Leaving the town clerk's office, Frankie overheard someone saying that they needed a builder like Old Chris had been, someone to help out with a little donated time. They couldn't afford to hire that kind of thing now. Couldn't even afford the materials.

"Cookbook," Frankie said as she turned to lock the door. The membership looked up at Frankie. Until that moment she had been invisible.

"One of those plastic-spined things that churches do?" asked someone. "We only have ninety-three families here. That's ninety-three recipes, half of them for crab cakes." Everybody laughed.

"No, not just those. The recipes would be the ones you need to know in order to live here. What you do when you are tired of the same old thing and you aren't ready for a ferry run?"

There was silence.

"Or get a good fish fry going for a hundred people? What did you do when the scallop fisherman caught the power cable and you and your freezers were without power? What about recipes from cooking for the couple of big houses of summer folks when they have a party?" she asked. "I'd do the organizing," she offered, wondering just what she was doing.

"Kind of risky. What if it didn't sell?" someone asked.

"I guess you'd be broke for sure," Frankie answered. "But think about it. You could put a picture of your lighthouse on it, sell it at the library, sell it at the ferry terminal, sell it in little bookstores on the mainland. Call it *The Hungry Islander*."

"How many islanders can there be?" asked someone.

"It wouldn't just be for folks who live on islands," said Frankie, "It would be for anyone who can imagine being on one. Cookbooks tell stories about being hungry."

"We could try out some of our final recipes at the Library Supper," someone said tentatively.

"I want to include Island Dressing," said Frankie. This was on page 218 in *Hazzard's* Chapter 12. "Connecting Rods."

"How in blazes do you know about Island Dressing?" hooted Lennie.

Wouldn't you like to know, thought Frankie. Aloud she said "Oh, I don't know. I must have overheard. Don't worry, Lennie, we'll save you the Raspberry Vinaigrette."

"I hate vinaigrette," snapped Lennie.

In *Hazzard's*, in Old Chris's script, the recipe ran like this:

Seasonal. Takes a full summer to prepare. First, help the people renting Lennie's cottage the day their faucet breaks and he's off on his boat. Then, wave hello as they head off to the quarry to swim. Finally, tell them after they miss the ferry how to hold one of the two reserve spaces next time. Wait. In August, when they leave, they will say, "What can we do with this?" They will have an unopened bag of flour, two ketchups and salad dressing. See what the neighbors find in the kitchens of their rentals. Give Lennie any raspberry vinaigrette.

Discard anything open. Get out the very big old clean mayo jars. Sample everything first. Combine and season to taste. There's no way to tell how it will turn out but it's always better than you'd guess. With a little luck there will be enough for the Ile du Nord Library dinner.

"You know, I could do that," said Elizabeth St. John. "I could organize a cookbook with our recipes."

Someone in the back called, "Frankie's boat's in the cove fair and square, Elizabeth, it's hers to fish." Everyone laughed.

"Might as well give it a chance," said Simon.

Weeks later, Frankie went to meet Simon at the ferry terminal for the outgoing afternoon boat. Cars and a few bikes and a plumbing and heating truck were starting to ease off the ferry ramp. Before Frankie could say anything, Simon called out to her from the line of island cars waiting to cross and then got out of the car to do a pirouette: "Do you like my mainland clothes," he called, giving a full view of his chinos and oxford blue shirt. He held a piece of paper with folded cash paper-clipped to it in the air. "I've got your list. There must be nearly a dozen kinds of pasta here."

Farfalle, fusilli, gemelli, penne smooth and rigate, campenelli—Frankie even loved the shape of their names. In *Hazzard's* she had sketch after sketch of each, transforming the shapes into beads: the illusion of twists and ridged cylinders caught inside transparent casings took on the suggestive qualities of carved bone and ancient sea life forms. When she abstracted the shapes of the pasta, ivory cane melted into encased designs and spirals and twists and ridges bloomed inside translucent glass layers.

"And," said the old postmaster, "I have the fuel filter and the piece of hose on the list. You sure you have the right part numbers?"

"Pretty sure, Simon—talked to the guy at the parts place a long time."

"Hey, Simon," a voice called. It was Lennie. "I need you to pick something up there for me, too. Got the time?"

"Sure. More Jeep trouble?"

"I ought to drive it straight into Quarry Pond." He gave Simon his own small wad of cash.

"Hey, Lennie," said Frankie, "I bet you keep getting the wrong alternator belt. Makes that little light flicker,"

"What do you know about engines?" asked Lennie.

"*Hazzard's*," she said.

"Hazzard? Who's that?"

"The manual," said Simon. "Old Chris's car repair manual." Lennie was already walking away, though, waving his hand in some cross between a dismissal and a farewell.

The cars started to move and Simon hopped back in his.

"You know, Frankie," he said, "Old Chris could never resist tangling with Lennie, either. But don't underestimate his bite."

Finding first gear, Simon asked, "Just what other stories does *Hazzard's* tell?"

"A new one every day, it seems," she said, backing away from the car as it started to roll.

Frankie looked at the dock, the boat, the ocean before her. A little peloton of day-trippers cycled past her toward the lighthouse. This was no wharf on a big inland lake with the opposite shore in view. Here she was, miles out into the Atlantic with a hundred recipes in her head, including Lucky's Casserole. What was Lucky's last chance to get it right? she wondered. And what do you think, Old Chris, if I tape a new soup recipe into our *Hazzard's*? The recipe she imagined had beans the color of carnelian beads and green penne rigate the shape of pistons. Mother's Bead Soup.

"What keeps you going out there on the island?" Gabe asked Frankie on the phone that night.

She had *Hazzard's* open on the counter. "Internal combustion," she said, looking at the recipe for Bead Soup, which was taped under Gasoline Engine Principles. "All this containment in a small space."

"Do you actually think you can make it through the winter in the middle of the Atlantic?" He sounded like he was afraid she would have to swim for it one day.

"I'll make do," she said, as she chopped celery into pieces that looked like half-moons of aventurine. She was deliberately not mentioning her car troubles. "How can I do a decent job of this cookbook if I'm not here?"

"You're really doing the *All-Can Can-Do Cookbook*?"

"The what? Oh, no—we're working on *The Hungry Islander*."

In Frankie's kitchen was a clipboard full of recipes. There were, indeed, several for crab cakes. Many of the recipes were eggy, given the island's hens, all laying eggs with shells of many hues from brown to pale green. The yolks were often a blazing, spectacular orange-red. There were Indonesian Rice Salad, Pepperoni Bread and cookies called Brambles. Test sheets for all of them were stacked in a pile on the bureau top. Everyone had started asking for the recipe for Old

Chris's Lightning Meringue Pie. Frankie couldn't quite figure out what the reference to its lightning was. The color of the lemon pie filling made vibrant by the egg yolks? The speed of its making? She would have to look for the recipe.

"This cookbook sounds terrific," Gabe said just before they hung up. "But why are you still there, really?"

"Because I just seem to have caught here, I guess."

"But do you belong there, Francia?"

Frankie wondered what the people on the island would say to that. "What do I know about belonging?" she answered, thinking then how much she would like to be on Ile du Nord long enough to see how the library's cookbook gamble paid off. She had plans for off-island book signing parties at bookstores in Blue Hill and Bar Harbor. She wanted to be around to go to those. And she wanted to see if the harbor froze over. It had once—there were pictures of it up at the ferry terminal. Most of all, she wanted simply to see how the colors changed here. And what she said was, "I just know that I can only make the beads I'm working on here. And I haven't exhausted my ideas yet."

For once, Gabe didn't mock her answer.

A new variation of Mother's Bead Soup was simmering and, as she hung up, she turned to add the spinach penne. She opened *Hazzard's* to "Fuel Feed Systems" and taped in Mother's Bead Soup, her first original recipe, beneath a disassembly diagram. Then, on impulse, Frankie settled at the table and picked up *Hazzard's* by each cover board, shaking it until the bound pages sagged away from the spine. The pie recipe had to be here. Clipped recipes, folded newspaper articles, receipts with notes scribbled on them, a flap of cardboard from a spark plug box that bore a parts number fell out. Sketches of beads that she had tucked in it fell out, too, along with a postcard from Gabe and the receipt for her registration at the bead show. Frankie shook it again and the two four leaf clovers fell out. Then, in the buckled gap between the cover of the spine and the stitched signatures of the book, she saw something lying flat. A manila envelope, small, like one keys might have come in from the hardware store. Folded inside it was Maggie's obituary, a newspaper article and a scrap of paper with a note that read *If you really want to try the Lightning Meringue Pie, make sure you use brown sugar in the meringue and island eggs in the lemon.* It was signed *love, M.* Beneath it were words written in Old Chris's now-familiar script that said *There's no one left to cook for.*

The newspaper clipping was from the Bangor paper—a photograph and a write-up of a reunion of Korean veterans, all in the Navy, all part of minesweeping operations. She recognized no one in the picture and none of the names in the caption—until she looked again at the name Nicky Zendo. Nicky Z. She flipped to the back of *Hazzard's.* There was his number. What else could she do, she thought, but follow the clues Old Chris had left behind to see if a voice on the other end of the line could tell her anything about her roommate.

A young woman answered the phone and, for an instant, Frankie was sure that Nicky Zendo had long since moved or died. The woman, though, seemed delighted to be asked for Mr. Zendo. "Dad," Frankie heard, "Dad, someone calling from Maine. A friend of Chris St. John."

It's a lot more complicated than friend thought Frankie. But friend wasn't entirely inaccurate.

Nicky wasn't surprised to learn that Old Chris was dead. "I hadn't heard from St. John for so long. I just figured," he said. "Did you know that we were in the Navy together, Korea?"

"I knew about Korea," she said, "but not anything else. Were you two stationed together?"

"He and I were in the dive team that cleared Wonsan Harbor of mines."

"Mines?" asked Frankie.

"A nightmare," said Nicky. "October—and cold. Snow on the hillsides of the harbor. Diving in our long johns to clear the sea lanes of mines because our wet suits kept floating us back up to the surface. I don't think I ever really warmed up. I still ache in the cold."

Frankie felt her bare feet on the chilly plank floor and heard the sounds of the Ile du Nord harbor in the background. She thought that maybe Nicky was crying, but the story seemed to be telling itself. She couldn't fully keep track of the cast of characters or the events in a Korean port she couldn't perfectly envision, but she leaned against the window sill and listened.

As Frankie pictured the story, she was hearing, she substituted the only harbor she knew, Ile du Nord's. She learned that on the Wonsan Harbor mission two ships hit mines after Chris and Nicky and the dive team thought they had cleared them all. The ships went down as the divers watched.

"One minute they're sailing in, flags waving, about to take the enemy port—and the next minute there's a hole in the *Pirate*'s hull and we're in the water after survivors. Then the other ship blows and sinks. A lot of men died, including St. Johns' best friend from basic. Another redhead. Found him floating in the sea on some debris." Nicky Zendo's voice both rasped and wavered now.

Frankie envisioned this little fishing village she knew made turbulent and lethal with mines.

"We'd put men in the water," said Nicky, "and then, when they were done, pulled them out. I was the sling man, slipping a loop around each swimmer and yanking him into the boat. Everybody knew staying in line and bobbing up when it was his turn was important. No second pass—too dangerous."

Frankie slid her back down the cupboards until she was sitting on the linoleum, cradling the phone between her ear and her shoulder. She was trying to picture the young man in Corinne's photograph exploding mines and searching for survivors.

"Two days after our ships sank and Chris found his friend dead, we went out to clear the sea-lanes of mines," Nicky said. "When the divers lined up to get snatched out of the water, St. John was last. And as our boat headed toward the end of the line of men, I saw him let himself sink back in the water. We picked up a little speed and veered off course to get him—and I yelled, 'Reach for it!' I don't know if he even heard me, but at the last instant he bobbed up like a redheaded seal and grabbed for it. For a second I thought he was going to swim out to sea."

Before they hung up, Nicky said, "Tell me, how did St. John die?" She couldn't answer.

After the phone call, Frankie let the receiver drop into her lap and reached behind her into the closest door and pulled out a box of cereal. She reached in for a handful and its crunch filled her ears. Later that afternoon, she went for a walk along the shore at low tide and picked a handful of the whitest periwinkle shells she could find. And, that night, she went through her beading notes till she found the book about ancient beading traditions that she used to take out of the library when she was an undergraduate and made a call to order it.

STROKE 4: EXHAUST

The only picture Frankie had ever seen of a string of Korean glass beads was in the book on ancient beads that had just arrived in the mail. There was a Korean tradition of stone beads called gogok beads that looked like commas or cashews or bear claws, pierced at one end—but Frankie didn't think she could manage a molten rendition that satisfied her. She propped the book open in her studio and worked on her version of the simple, centuries-old string of a dozen beads: four big dark honey-brown beads spaced between eight smaller ones in dark burnt yellow and amber-green—all nearly opaque in the way beach glass is battered past transparency after its time in the ocean. They were, in a sense, easy and unembellished beads, except for her desire to get their particular dark near-opacity and their colors and their shapes perfect. She filled a coffee can with attempts. None of this was destined for the bead show.

This was September and the pieces she had made for the New England Bead Show rolled and coiled like rockweed on the shore. Creating necklaces from focal beads entangled in beaded ropes had given her a way to anchor the old talismans in her new work. Strung on necklaces made with strands of natural fiber beaded in bits of flameworked amber or olive or lapis glass, they looked like they had been delivered with the tide. Booth #373 would be like nothing she had envisioned when the ferry first delivered her to Ile du Nord. By September, she had collected dozens of recipes for the cookbook and the island was going to try them out at the library dinner.

Frankie still didn't know how Old Chris St. John came to be lost at sea.

"Why does it even matter, Frankie?" asked Gabe. They were on the phone and he was trying to convince her to come back to Ohio. "I'd like to see you more often. And from what you've said, it's not easy to get on there."

"It matters because Old Chris and I seem to be working from the same manual," she said.

"Are you set for that bead show?" he asked.

"Nearly," she said, picturing empty yellow butane canisters that had filled the box by her worktable over the last months. The New England Bead show would be a verdict on her island studio, but she felt ready for it.

Then he asked the question she knew he would. "What comes after the show?"

Frankie could struggle her way through the winter on her clerk's salary, but beyond that she would have to take her chances with what came of the bead show. If she still felt like a bead artist after spending a week among other bead artists, the answer was to buy the new torch and figure out how to launch a bead business from a Maine island. "We'll see," she answered.

"Maybe I'd feel better about what you're up to if you weren't on a remote island channeling a long-dead, reluctant fisherman with a knack for making pies and alienating people."

"Are you challenging my taste in friends?" she asked, amazed again at Gabe's devastating abilities to sum up her life.

One Friday afternoon not too long after Labor Day, when Frankie arrived to help set up for the next day's Ile du Nord library supper, she found the men already outside in the parking lot setting up fifty-gallon drums that had been cut lengthwise and transformed into open grills. The evening before, she had baked pie shells for her own go at providing the lemon meringue legend for the island's big supper. And she had spent the morning at Corinne's.

She and Corinne had been cooking up the entire contents of Corinne's freezer: its compressor had given out. Vast quantities of Harvard Beets, Elizabeth's recipe, were now destined for the Library Supper—and large quantities of blueberries were being turned into pies. Frankie and Corinne were taking the whole freezer problem in stride—until one of the blueberry pies slipped off the table and suddenly became a disaster, too. They bent to clean it up—the kitchen already stained in beet and blueberry juices and the sink full and the freezer still leaking a little from its great thaw. What came over them then, Frankie couldn't quite say, but Corinne dished out two bowls of the freezer's melting vanilla ice cream and took a spatula to one of the surviving warm pies and announced, "Blueberry Disaster Sundaes." And then they did in all the pies. The idea had seemed brilliant at the time: big chunks of fragrant, fresh blueberry pie tossed in with vanilla ice cream to serve at the island dinner.

"If Cookie Dough Ice Cream is a hit," said Corinne, "this will have everyone at the Library Dinner vying for the last serving. This one goes in the cookbook." It had smelled so gorgeous—warm pie, melting ice cream—she and Corinne had eaten a double share.

Frankie arrived at the library that afternoon energized by Disaster Sundaes. Simon waved to her as she approached, but the others kept at their work. He and Jacko and Lennie had been doing this job for years, she thought, leaning the bike against the clapboarding of the building. And Old Chris would have been here with them on a day like this, helping to set up. These were the men who would know the answer to how Old Chris died, she thought. She couldn't ask Corinne. Maybe this was the time.

"Thought you might need another hand," she said, beginning to bolt together planking for the picnic tables and wondering if she would be shooed away again.

There was no chatter for a few minutes. Lennie seemed to be on his good behavior. Simon must have talked to him, Frankie thought.

Then Lennie's sharp voice broke in on the sounds of benches being assembled. "Why did you come here in the first place? Did you really come all this way for Old Chris's chicken coop?" he asked.

There was the Lennie she knew, thought Frankie. "I wanted to set up a studio for my torch," she answered.

"Yeah," said Lennie, "that's what you told my wife. But why here?"

Frankie kept her eyes on her wrench and torqued another bolt tight. Because I was having a bad day and I was told this island was a gem, she thought. Because I thought I knew about islands and ferries because I looked out at them everyday on Lake Champlain. And then she shrugged, saying "Everybody gets caught somewhere."

Work had stopped, but it didn't feel like a coffee break. They are trying to figure out what to make of me, Frankie thought. She cast a glance at Simon for support, but instead he said, though not unkindly, "Really, Frankie, why did you pick here, out of all the possible places in the world?"

This was no place to tell stories about bead shops and take-out lunches and old boyfriends. Or notebooks full of sketches of ancient Phoenician beads and polyhedrals of lapis lazuli—and full of her own plans for beads that might emerge from her time bent to the torch, the flame roaring inches from her fingers. "Just lucky," she answered, knowing that that was as accurate as she could get and that whatever her answer was, it wouldn't be answer enough. So these are Old Chris's friends, she thought. Formidable. This was the time to ask her own question.

"How did Old Chris die?"

Everyone looked caught off-guard.

"Drowned," said Simon. "Presumed drowned. The summer after Maggie died. We found his rowboat, tied to the buoy, empty. No note."

"What does it matter now?" asked Lennie.

Simon kept going. "When he didn't show up at the library dinner, everyone thought he was just mad."

"Mad?" asked Frankie.

"He and Lennie had had a little blowout the day before. I thought he was just cooling off."

"What happened had nothing to do with me telling him it was his fault my generator light kept coming on," said Lennie.

"You told him he was no mechanic at all," said Jacko, "and that if he had been, Lucky would still be alive. You told him he didn't need to show up with his big pies for the supper."

No one left to cook for, thought Frankie. Aloud, she said, "This has something to do with Lucky?"

"Something to do with Lucky?" said Lennie. "It was Old Chris who let Lucky die."

Simon quietly said, "It wasn't Old Chris who decided to go out fishing that day, Lennie. Lucky was hauling too close to shore. And it was too windy a day for fishing Stonecutters Cove. Engine quit, is what I think. No time to drop anchor. He went into the rocks."

"It was Old Chris's fault the engine quit!" Lennie was angry. "Wasn't that a Chevy engine he dropped in that boat?" asked Jacko.

"Chrysler, '42 Chrysler," said Frankie, the notes in *Hazzard's* as familiar to her as any recipe. "And Lucky needed to get himself a new fuel filter. Part 1749A."

"How in hell do you know," Lennie snapped, and then said, "but it doesn't matter. He might have been foolhardy to go out, but it was Old Chris who let him die. He should have tried to help him. He knew the shape of that engine better than anyone."

"Come on, Lennie," Simon interjected, "Admit it. Lucky took lots of risks. It was a hard chance that he was ever really going to make it. Didn't we all half-expect to look out one day and see Lucky's boat turning in slow circles by itself and no Lucky left to tell the story?"

"And did you expect to see Old Chris's boat moored to the buoy, empty?" asked Frankie.

"Why do you care?" Lennie demanded. "Nothing can change that he left Lucky to go it alone. Heartless old bastard. Remember him rowing out and dumping all Maggie's cookware the day of her funeral?"

"Maybe there are a lot of ways to mourn," Frankie said.

"You aren't even from around here," said Lennie. "It's none of your business."

"I was over there that morning," said Simon, "when he spread the tarp across the linoleum and started piling it with her things in the kitchen. He was a grieving man, Lennie."

"You were there?" asked Lennie. "You never said!"

"Why didn't you go out with him?" Frankie asked Simon, but Simon didn't answer.

"Nothing changes the fact that he left Lucky to go it alone," Lennie hammered back.

Frankie turned from Simon to Lennie. "Seems like maybe all of you left Old Chris to go it alone, too."

"Old Piss wanted it that way!"

"Is that why he fixed your jeep and made you Lightning Meringue Pie?"

"He came back from the Navy strange, Frankie," said Jacko. "Didn't want anything to do with fishing. Kept a distance. We didn't know what to make of him."

Lennie spun on Frankie. "Taking care of our recipes! I bet you don't even know how to cook! Cassie may have died and left you town clerk, but you have no business trying to tell us stories about things you weren't part of. Just what do you think you know?"

The look on Simon's face froze. He thinks I'm going to blurt out something about Corinne and Old Chris, she thought. When she opened her mouth, she found herself saying, "Wonsan Harbor is what I know." She hadn't expected to tell them about the Korean fishing harbor scattered with small islands and filled with mines. About the Navy trying to take the port. Until this moment it hadn't fully dawned on her that Old Chris had never told the island any of what Zendo had told her. Having them understand this piece of Old Chris's life seemed important just then. This had been her opening to find out what happened to him, maybe this was theirs.

"I know Old Chris swam in the cold Sea of Japan to clear out the mines," said Frankie. "During the day his unit cut mine cables and exploded mines and sometimes retrieved the wounded and the dead. I know the harbor was afloat with diesel and dead fish after the explosions and the stench was terrible. I know that at night, on patrols, Old Chris scouted for North Koreans re-mining the sea-lanes. Scouting meant blowing them and their fishing boats out of the water with machine guns when he found them."

"Wonsan?" said Simon. "Wonsan? He never once mentioned it to me. How do you know?"

Simon sat down on one of the completed benches. "How did you find this out," he began, but Lennie blew.

"Clear out of here," Lennie said. "Old Chris is dead and gone. We don't want to hear your stories."

Frankie had already stood up from the picnic tables, sliding her tote over her shoulder and righting the bike from where it leaned against the library. She had said more than she meant to.

As she walked the bike across the gravel driveway, she heard Simon saying something to Lennie. Something about admitting it was time to let things go. Maybe giving things a chance. And then as she pushed off on the bike, she heard Simon yell, "I'll be over in the morning to take you to the Van Man."

Frankie had returned to the kitchen on Quarry Road from the library parking lot needing to take the torch to something. And now she smelled the singeing of her eyelashes and eyebrows and felt an almost exuberant desire to blast back. Three huge lemon meringue pies sat waiting to have their meringue caramelized to glory and the oven with its tricky pilot had just blown her across the room. This is the last straw, thought Frankie. She slammed the oven door.

Frankie wasn't up for another go at lighting the oven. The pies were before her, brown sugar meringue six inches thick, rising in peaks and waves. Beneath it, lemon filling made with eggs from island backyard chickens blazed it into color as vibrant as sunset. If she were going to brown this glorious meringue, there was nothing for it but to torch it. She fished in the drawer and came up with Old Chris's gas nozzle. She understood suddenly why Old Chris kept it in the kitchen bureau and what the blast marks outlining spheres across the top of the bureau—scorched as if by lightning—came from. They were from Old Chris's Lightning Meringue Pie, meringue caramelized in a blue flame from a soldering torch.

Frankie retrieved her own yellow canister from the studio and ignited the flow of gas, its faint smell filling the air. An almost invisible flame shot blue and yellow and, sometimes, needles of lightning. Comfort, thought Frankie, is sometimes a thing that shoots fire. The flame wuthered like the sounds of wind catching the edge of the house and she burnt a trench straight down the first pie as she misjudged the angles and the smell of scorched sugar filled her nostrils. It was beautiful. The bureau's varnish darkened at the rim of the pan, flaming the grain of the wood into visibility, adding her scorch rings to Old Chris's. She practiced wielding lightning on this first pie, then moved on, newly expert on pies and compressed gas. Frankie let the bolt of flame caramelize the remaining two.

All of this was risky, thought Frankie—broken-down cars, lost lovers, living on a knob of spruce and granite eight miles out to sea, The New England Bead Show, turning up at the library supper. The flame was just a way of talking about that to herself. When she awoke the next morning, she knew there was no way around what was going to have to happen, particularly if she wanted to deliver the pies to the island supper on her own. She had the fuel filter for her old car, but not the tools to install it. When Simon came back with the fuel filter, he had said that the man at the parts store had asked if he wanted the special wrench used for replacing the filter. And the parts specialist mentioned something about a gauge to measure the pressure in the fuel line. Apparently cars had changed a little in the nearly fifty years since *Hazzard's* had been published. Thirty dollars for the filter, sixty for the wrench. Who knew how much for the pressure gauge or how even to use it. This was clearly more than a matter of assembly.

So here it was, the ignominy of being towed. "Mind the brake," said Simon when he arrived on Quarry Road, attaching the tow chain to her bumper and then to the trailer hitch on his little truck. "That hill is steep. It's mostly down hill to the wharf, but let's not end up in the drink." Frankie hoped her bumper would hold.

She cringed a little at the small spectacle of their tandem travel—which went smoothly enough with a little lurch-and-drag action as she and Simon tried to coordinate. One of the women she bought eggs from waved from beside her mailbox. Three kids headed for Corinne's stood at the side of the road to watch the little procession, one pumping his arm beside his ear to get them to beep their horns. Simon complied, Frankie followed suit. Lennie's Jeep pulled over to give them room to maneuver and he waved.

And then it dawned on her. This wasn't the ride of shame, but a rite of passage: getting towed to the Van Man. This was an Ile du Nord summer parade and Simon was, probably not for the first time, Grand Marshall. Frankie clicked the ignition key to the on position and slipped in a CD. Any parade needed music and a little Celtic fiddle would have to do. The reception the tiny caravan got at the wharf was a bit like being greeted at the finishing line. Toomey, who was loading traps, came over to inspect her bumper—which was never going to be quite the same—and to ask Simon how she had handled the last downhill curve.

So this was an island apprenticeship, she thought as she sat on the wharf waiting for her car to be fixed: a blue flame, a clogged fuel filter, a Korean harbor, a car repair manual, a lost lobster boat, drowned spatulas and egg beaters, pasta pouring from the box, shells along the shore. She was, it seemed, alive and well on Ile du Nord after all.

That night, the library parking lot was full when she pulled in and the building was all but over-flowing. Three men she recognized from the lobster pound were just headed into the side door. Here they all are, she thought, the people who live on Ile du Nord. All the faces newly familiar to her. Among them, Old Chris's friends— and hers. She held them all briefly in mind, a constellation of islanders. She was pierced by a sense of them all—caught here for reasons of their own. As similar as shells rolled together in rockweed—or as distinct as a pocketful of old beads: carnelian prayer beads and Venetian trade beads and ancient eye beads and neon beads inspired by lobster floats, gathered together to rattle along in company. In the back seat, the debris of recipe test sheets and, safely in open boxes on the floor, two Lightning Meringue pies.

Frankie was twisting around in her seat and reaching for them when Simon startled her by knocking on her car window. "I didn't know if you would come, Frankie," he said. "The Blueberry Disaster Sundaes are already the hit of the evening. Corinne's been telling the story."

"Is it safe to bring these in?" Frankie asked, rolling the window down and handing him one of the cresting waves of brown sugar meringue.

Simon held out his hands. "And so, Lightning Meringue Pie has come back to us again. Is this recipe going into *The Hungry Islander*?"

"No," she said. "This one belongs to Quarry Road."

"This cookbook you're making, old friend, may take longer than you anticipated," said Simon. "Why not give us a little time?"

Weeks later, Frankie headed west on the ferry in her mainland clothes, the trip across the eight-mile stretch of ocean taking on an odd formality. She had done Simon's ferry-boarding shimmy in front of the mirror this morning in her batik skirt. Around her neck, her old torch-made bead. Now she stood with her back against her car. The weather had cooled in spite of the bright early October sun. Just a ferry run to town with directions to the airport in Simon's handwriting spread out on the passenger's seat. What would her brother say about her chosen geography when she brought him back on the ferry, she wondered.

The morning boat cleared the first buoy where a seagull rested and she listened to its deep clangor, the sounds of lost eggbeaters and lost souls. She leaned over the rail as the ferry turned at the buoy and the buoy pitched in the boat's wake. Reaching into her pocket, she scooped up a string of dark honey-brown and burnt yellow and amber-green beads, half dozen bleached periwinkles and a small handful of loose beads—neon beads that echoed lobster floats, beads etched like barnacles, beads the color of wet granite and mussel shells. "Hi there, old friend," she said, letting the tiny talismans drop. "If there are many chances to get this right, let's take this one."

2012
PRESS 53
OPEN AWARDS ANTHOLOGY

POETRY

POETRY JUDGE Tom Lombardo is poetry series editor for Press 53. He is a poet, essayist, and freelance writer who lives in Midtown Atlanta. Tom's poems have appeared in journals in the U.S., the U.K., Canada, and India, including *Southern Poetry Review, Ambit, Subtropics, Hampden-Sydney Poetry Review, Aethlon: The Journal of Sports Literature, Atlanta Review, New York Quarterly, Chrysalis Reader,* and others. His nonfiction has appeared in *Chrysalis Reader, Spectrum* magazine, *Leisure* magazine and has been nominated for a Pushcart Prize. He was editor of *After Shocks: The Poetry of Recovery,* an anthology featuring 152 poems by 115 poets from 15 nations. His criticism has been published in *New Letters, North Carolina Literary Review,* and *South Carolina Review.* He earned a B.S. from Carnegie-Mellon University, an M.S. from Ohio University, and an M.F.A. from Queens University of Charlotte.

NOTE FROM THE JUDGE: "Simply put, this poet has presented three wonderful poems of great insight and clarity. She examines loss through three distinct episodes along her path to recovery, sharpening focus and deepening the reader's emotional experience skillfully with metaphor and other figurative language. Each poem unfolds from imagery to revelations of hidden truths of this life—and possibly the next."

FIRST PRIZE POETRY:
Dominique Traverse Locke received her B.A. in English from Virginia Intermont College where she served as editor of the college's literary magazine, and received her MFA in Creative Writing from Queens University of Charlotte. While at Queens, Dominique studied with poets Cathy Smith Bowers, Alan Michael Parker, Sally Keith,

Claudia Rankine and many other masters of their craft. She has been publishing work in literary magazines such as *The Sow's Ear Poetry Review, Barely South Review,* and other fine publications regularly since 2006. Dominique's first collection of poems, a chapbook entitled *The Goodbye Child,* was published by Aldrich Publishing in late spring of 2012. Her first full-length collection of poems, *No More Hard Times,* is forthcoming from Alabaster Leaves Press. She resides in the Appalachian Mountains of southwest Virginia with her husband, the poet, David Alan Locke.

SECOND PRIZE POETRY:

Peg Bresnahan is the author of *Chasing Light,* a book of poetry. She is currently working on another manuscript. Her poetry has been published in U.S. journals and online. Poems have recently appeared in *The Southern Poetry Review, The South Carolina Review,* and *The Main Street Rag.* She has an MFA in poetry from Vermont College. Ten years ago, Peg moved from the Door County peninsula in Wisconsin, to Cedar Mountain, North Carolina, where she lives with her husband, sculptor Dan Bresnahan, and their Doberman and two cats.

HONORABLE MENTION POETRY:

David Cazden has been poetry editor for *Miller's Pond* magazine for 6 years, has one book, *Moving Picture* (Word Press, 2005). He has poems recent or forthcoming in *Passages North, Nimrod* (Semi Finalist for the Pablo Neruda Prize), *Fugue* (2nd place winner of the Rod McFarland Poetry Prize), *The Crab Creek Review, Kestrel, William and Mary Review, The Louisville Review,* and elsewhere. David received an Al Smith Fellowship for poetry from the Kentucky Arts Council in 2008.

FLASH FICTION

Flash Fiction judge Meg Pokrass published her debut collection of flash fiction, *Damn Sure Right*, with Press 53 in 2011. Her short novel, *The Sticky Lust of Hummingbirds,* has recently been commissioned for screenplay adaptation. Her stories have appeared in over 150 literary magazines including *PANK, Mississippi Review, The Literarian, storySouth, Smokelong Quarterly, Wigleaf's Top 50 Fictions* of 2010 and 2012, *The Rumpus, McSweeney's Internet Tendency,* and others. Meg creates and runs the Fictionaut Five Author Interview series for *Fictionaut* and is launching *Uncaged Interviews,* a new series with Best-selling Author/Book Reviewer, Caroline Leavitt.

Note from the judge: " 'Mastering the Art of French Cooking' is inventive, playful, bittersweet and surprising. It offers the reader a huge three-course meal in just a few unforgettable bites—pulling us in with a short, sly recipe of humor blended with pain and self-loathing whisked with bacon-lust, the end of trust, and more than a pinch of love gone sour and deadly."

First Prize Flash Fiction:
Art Taylor's short fiction has appeared in *Ellery Queen's Mystery Magazine, Barrelhouse, Needle: A Magazine of Noir,* and *North American Review,* and online at *Fiction Weekly, Mysterical-E, PANK, Plots With Guns, Prick of the Spindle,* and *SmokeLong Quarterly,* among other publications. "A Voice from the Past" was an honorable mention for the 2010 *Best American Mystery Stories.* "Rearview Mirror" won the 2011 Derringer Award for Best Novelette, and "A Drowning at Snow's Cut" won the 2012 Derringer Award for Best Long Story. He also received a 2012 Strauss Fellowship from the Arts

Council of Fairfax County. In addition to his own fiction, Art reviews mysteries and thrillers for the *Washington Post* and contributes frequently to *Mystery Scene Magazine*. For more information, visit www.arttaylorwriter.com.

SECOND PRIZE FLASH FICTION:
Nahal S. Jamir earned her Ph.D. from Florida State University. Her work has been published in or is forthcoming in *The South Carolina Review*, *Jabberwock Review*, *Meridian*, *The Los Angeles Review*, *Crab Orchard Review*, *Carolina Quarterly*, *Ruminate Magazine*, and *Passages North*.

HONORABLE MENTION FLASH FICTION:
Amanda Pauley is a fiction writer from Elliston, Virginia. She began writing fiction as an English major at Virginia Polytechnic Institute and State University and continued through a Master of Arts in Liberal Studies degree at Hollins University. She spent a brief period as a freelance writer, publishing articles in magazines including, *Blue Ridge Traditions*, *Virginia Tourist*, *Dulcimer Players News*, *Blue Ridge Country*, *and Prime Living*. Amanda has been a finalist multiple times in the Press 53 Open Awards and she won first place for a story in the 2011 Press 53 Open Awards. She was also a finalist for the 2012 Thomas Wolfe Fiction Prize. She has been published twice, and has another story forthcoming, in the *Clinch Mountain Review*. This fall Amanda was thrilled to be able to return to Hollins University in the Master of Fine Arts in Creative Writing program with the help of a Richard Dillard Scholarship, as well as a Roanoke Pen Women Scholarship.

SHORT STORY

SHORT STORY JUDGE **Clifford Garstang** is the author of the novel in stories, *What the Zhang Boys Know* (Press 53, 2012), and the prize-winning short story collection *In an Uncharted Country* (Press 53, 2009). His work has appeared in *Bellevue Literary Review*, *Blackbird*, *Virginia Quarterly Review*, *Cream City Review*, *Tampa Review*, *The Los Angeles Review*, and elsewhere, and has received Distinguished Mention in the Best American Series. He won the 2006 *Confluence* Fiction Prize and the 2007 *GSU Review* Fiction Prize. He has received fellowships from the Virginia Center for the Creative Arts and the Sewanee Writers' Conference. In addition to degrees in law and public administration, he holds an MFA from Queens University of Charlotte and is the co-founder and editor of *Prime Number Magazine*.

NOTE FROM THE JUDGE: "Everything about this story—the title, the controlling metaphor, the setting, the dialogue—is fresh and fun, and yet the story manages to delve into the universal mysteries of relationships and what is knowable."

FIRST PRIZE SHORT STORY: **Kathryn Etters Lovatt** earned her MA in creative writing from Hollins University. Her work has appeared in a number of anthologies and literary magazines, most recently in *The Petigru Review*, *Main Street Rag*, and *MoonShine Review*. Awards include the North Carolina Writers Network Doris Betts Prize, the South Carolina Writers Workshop Carrie McCray Memorial Award , and the 2013 Individual Artist Fellowship for prose by the South Carolina Arts Commission. She is a Virginia Center for the Creative Arts fellow, and both her poetry and fiction have received Pushcart Prize nominations. Before returning to her hometown of Camden, South Carolina in 2007, she lived, studied and wrote in Virginia, North Carolina, New Jersey, Jakarta, Hong Kong and London.

SECOND PRIZE SHORT STORY:
Alison Morse's poetry and short prose have been published widely, most recently in *Water~Stone Review*, *Moment Magazine*, *MNArtists.org*, *Natural Bridge* and *The Pedestal*. *The Strength of Mothers*, her stories about Kenyan activist Wahu Kaara, were published by the Women Peacemakers Program at the Joan Kroc Institute for Peace and Justice in 2012. Alison also teaches English to new immigrants and is the founder and director of TalkingImageConnection, a reading series that brings together writers, visual artists and new audiences.

HONORABLE MENTION SHORT STORY:
Gary V. Powell's stories have been widely published in print and online literary journals, including the *Briar Cliff Review*, *The Thomas Wolfe Review*, *The Dead Mule School of Southern Literature*, and *The Newport Review*. In addition, several of his stories have placed or been selected as finalists in national contests. Most recently, his story "Home Free" won an Honorable Mention in the 2011 Newport Review Flash Fiction Contest, and his story "The Fire Next Time" received an Honorable Mention in the New Millennium Spring 2012 Flash Fiction contest. His first novel, *Lucky Bastard*, is currently available through Main Street Rag Press at www.mainstreetrag.com/GPowell.html.

CREATIVE NONFICTION

CREATIVE NONFICTION JUDGE **Tracy Crow** is nonfiction editor at *Prime Number Magazine* and the author of the memoir, *Eyes Right, Confessions from a Woman Marine* (University of Nebraska Press, 2012), in which she chronicles her life as a Marine journalist during the groundbreaking 1980s. Her essays have appeared in the *Missouri Review, Mississippi Review, Puerto del Sol, Literary Mama,* and others, and have been nominated for three Pushcart Prizes. Her short story, "Natural Selection," based on events from her life as a Marine, was anthologized in the Press 53 collection, *Home of the Brave: Stories in Uniform* (2009). She is a graduate of the M.F.A. program at Queens University of Charlotte in North Carolina. As assistant professor of creative writing at Eckerd College in St. Petersburg, Florida, she teaches journalism and creative nonfiction, and advises the award-winning, nationally recognized college newspaper, *The Current.*

NOTE FROM THE JUDGE: "From the opening paragraph, 'Lies That Bind' seduces with sensory and sensual language. I knew immediately this essay would be a contender, and later, despite reading a number of excellent entries, this essay continued to resonate because of its attention to language and its haunting themes about identity and self-preservation. In 'Lies That Bind,' the writer so artfully weaves her narrative with her mother's that readers are rewarded with a provocative, even voyeuristic, glimpse at an extremely dark and complicated relationship built years and years on lies."

CREATIVE NONFICTION FIRST PRIZE:
Leslie Tucker, a Detroit escapee, lives on a South Carolina mountainside and refuses to divulge its exact location. She is an avid hiker and zip liner, a dedicated yogi, an ACBL Life Master in Sanctioned Bridge, and enjoys anything that requires a helmet. She holds degrees in business and music. Her work has appeared in

the 2010 and 2012 Press 53 Anthologies, *The Tarnished Anthology, Fiction Fix, So to Speak, Shenandoah Magazine, Prime Number Magazine* and *The Baltimore Review.*

CREATIVE NONFICTION SECOND PRIZE:
Sandell Morse lives on the coat of Maine with her husband and two standard poodles. She holds a Master's Degree in Liberal Studies from Dartmouth College and a Master's Degree in English (fiction writing) from the University of New Hampshire. She has taught at the University of New Hampshire and at the University of Maine, Farmington. Her short stories and nonfiction have appeared in *Green Mountains Review, Ploughshares, New England Review, Boston Fiction Review,* and others. Sandell has been a Tennessee Williams Scholar at the Sewanee Writers' Conference, a finalist in the Ploughshares Robie Macauley Fellowship Award, received a nomination for a Pushcart prize, been a fellow at the Vermont Studio Colony and at the Virginia Center for the Creative Arts, where she serves on the Board of Directors. A recent excerpt from her memoir, *Girl Wrapped in a Curtain,* won the Michael Steinberg essay prize and appears in *Fourth Genre.* Find Sandell on Facebook and Linkedin. Her website is sandellmorse.com, and you can read her blog at sandellmorse.blogspot.com.

CREATIVE NONFICTION HONORABLE MENTION:
Hannah Karena Jones is an Assistant Editor at Transaction Publishers. She has had work appear or forthcoming in *Inside Pennsylvania, The Honors Review, The Stillwater Review,* and *Weave Magazine,* among others. Her work has been awarded second place in *The Baltimore Review* Creative Non-Fiction Contest, Honorable Mention in the *Writer's Digest* Young Adult Fiction Competition, and was a finalist in Biographile's Short Memoir Competition. "What to Expect While Grieving for Your Father" first appeared in *The Susquehanna Review.* Her book, *Byberry State Hospital,* is forthcoming from Arcadia Publishing and she maintains a blog at thewwaitingroom.wordpress.com.

NOVELLA

NOVELLA JUDGE **Robin Miura** has worked in publishing for 12 years, first as a production editor for Oxford University Press and for the past nine years as a freelance editor, proofreader, publishing consultant, and writing coach for publishing companies and individual authors. She has worked with all types of books—from academic and educational to self-help— but her passion is literary fiction and creative nonfiction. Robin has edited a novel and memoir series for Press 53 and edited the two most recent Fred Bonnie Award–winning novels for River City Publishing: *Shrapnel* by Marie Manilla and *Girl from Soldier Creek* by Patricia Foster. You can find out more about Robin and her work at alturl.com/qfrhj.

NOTE FROM THE JUDGE: "From its first paragraph, *Hazzard's* plunges us into the mind and emotions of its protagonist, Frankie, and we go along on her adventure of seeking change and respite from her everyday life by moving to a small island off the coast of Maine where she plans to hone her skills as a glass bead artist. The author treats us to vibrant imagery of the coast, the village, the shells, the light, the ocean, and the color-laden beads of Frankie's craft—all set against the complex relationships among and between the residents of this isolated town. Here Frankie begins the work of sorting out what she should jettison from her own complicated past and what she should retain and create for herself going forward. This is a masterfully told story of self-discovery and self-reliance."

FIRST PRIZE NOVELLA:
Stephanie DeGhett is a fiction writer and poet with recent fiction in *The Missouri Review* and *Confrontation*. She has fiction due out in *Southern Humanities Review*. Her recent poetry has appeared in *Poetry East, Harpur Palate and Slipstream*. Her poem "Anthracite Dreams" was an award winner in the *Spoon River Review* Poetry Contest. She teaches in the Creative Writing BFA Program at SUNY Potsdam.

CPSIA information can be obtained at www.ICGtesting.com
Printed in the USA
BVOW032257311012

304390BV00001B/14/P